The Modern Patriot

A Voter's Guide To U.S. Energy Policy

Thomas G. Komjathy

Bloomington, IN   Milton Keynes, UK

authorHOUSE®

AuthorHouse™
1663 Liberty Drive, Suite 200
Bloomington, IN 47403
www.authorhouse.com
Phone: 1-800-839-8640

AuthorHouse™ UK Ltd.
500 Avebury Boulevard
Central Milton Keynes, MK9 2BE
www.authorhouse.co.uk
Phone: 08001974150

First published by AuthorHouse 8/21/2006

ISBN: 1-4259-5114-7 (sc)

Printed in the United States of America
Bloomington, Indiana

This book is printed on acid-free paper.

To Kim, for her reliable support and wisdom,
and to the teachers, colleagues, and friends who have
focused the lens through which I see the world.

Contents

Useful Unit Conversions

Quantity	Base Unit	Equivalence
Energy	1 BTU	= 251.96 calorie (cal)[1]
		= 0.000293 kilowatt-hour (kWh)
		= 2.52×10^{-8} tonnes of oil equivalent (toe)
		= 3.60×10^{-8} tonnes of coal equivalent (tce)
		= 1054.19 joule (J)
		= 6.59×10^{21} electron-volt (eV)
Power	1 BTU/hr	= 0.000393 horsepower (hp)
		= 0.293 watt (W)
		= 8.33×10^{-5} ton of refrigeration
		= 0.007 kWh per day

---

[1] The thermochemical calorie, shown in this table, should not be confused with the nutritional calorie (commonly listed on food labels). One nutritional calorie (Cal) = 1,000 thermochemical calories (cal).

Foreword

What are the defining characteristics of patriotism? Patriots take action of national significance. They face important challenges head-on when it is easier or more comfortable to look the other way. They do these things for the love of their families, their neighbors, and their country. Whom do you consider to be a patriot according to this definition? Perhaps you think of the passengers of United Flight 93, Dr. Martin Luther King, Jr., or the student protesters at Tiananmen Square. Their lives were the archetypes of patriotism.

Who will be the next patriots? Must they necessarily be identified on a battlefield? Or is there another theater in which their convictions can be revealed? The modern patriot will be he who seeks to understand the great challenges facing our nation. He will find the time, against the force of an ever-quickening pace of life, to learn about complex issues. He will not take comfort in the thought that others will find the solutions for him. He will not succumb to the temptation to withhold his vote as a protest against "our broken system". He will not choose on the basis of sensationalism. Rather, he will consider it a duty to be informed, to have an opinion, and to participate fully in our democracy.

What is your reasonable service to those who have gone before you, those who have given their lives to preserve your freedom? It is the modern patriotism that honors their memory.

Introduction

Have you ever found yourself thinking about any of the following questions?

- Are today's gas prices the result of gouging by oil companies, and will they ever go back to "normal"?

- Is global warming *really* happening, and if so, how urgent is the need for action?

- When, if ever, will hydrogen-powered cars become practical?

- On the whole, is nuclear power good or bad for society?

- Why has the U.S. chosen not to ratify the Kyoto Protocol treaty on climate change, while 160 other countries have[1]?

- Will the U.S. government allow oil exploration in the Arctic National Wildlife Refuge?

- What caused "the blackout" of 2003, and what has been done to prevent it from happening again?

If the answer is "yes", then you have an interest in energy policy, perhaps even without knowing it. This book is meant for you. **Its purpose is to provide you with a non-partisan layperson's guide to energy issues currently facing the U.S., with a view towards helping you to become an informed "consumer" of energy policy.** Energy policy is coupled with politics, and with modern politics comes a deluge of information that can (and unfortunately is sometimes intended to) overwhelm the voter. With ever-increasing demands on our time and attention, we don't have the energy or resources to differentiate fact from partial truth from fiction. You may recall, for example, the 2004 presidential election during which we were bombarded with advertisements from one group of swift-boat veterans after another, some affirming that Senator John Kerry was a war hero, and others vehemently denying it. In such cases, our human nature is to tune out the noise and go with our instincts.

Nevertheless, ignoring complex issues does not make them go away. Energy supply is one of the most important issues facing our country, and shouldn't be left to "gut-feeling" decisions. Mid-term elections are coming in November, 2006, and you will likely hear many different ideas about where we should be headed with respect to energy and what priority it should receive compared with other issues of national importance. If you doubt this, please consider the following excerpt from President Bush's 2006 State of the Union Address[2]:

"So tonight, I announce the Advanced Energy Initiative -- a 22-percent increase in clean-energy research -- at the Department of Energy, to push for breakthroughs in two vital areas. To change how we power our homes and offices, we will invest more in zero-emission coal-fired plants, revolutionary solar and wind technologies, and clean, safe nuclear energy.

We must also change how we power our automobiles. We will increase our research in better batteries for hybrid and electric cars, and in pollution-free cars that run on hydrogen. We'll also fund additional research in cutting-edge methods of producing ethanol, not just from corn, but from wood chips and stalks, or switch grass. Our goal is to make this new kind of ethanol practical and competitive within six years."

Similar attention exists at the State level. For example, in April, 2006, Michigan Governor Jennifer Granholm launched an on-line petition *"calling on President Bush to support a cap on excessive oil company profits"*[3]. Like it or not, it seems that energy policy is at the forefront of our national attention. If you read this book, you can expect to develop a solid foundation upon which to build your own opinions about such issues. You will also have greater confidence when marking your ballot, making personal lifestyle choices, or even deciding on investments.

Energy Supply – Today's Most Pressing Policy Issue?

If we were to survey Americans about the biggest challenges currently facing our country, the ones most likely to impact our quality of life and that of future generations, what would be the results? The list would probably include issues such as the course of American military engagements, the rising costs of health care and higher education, the loss of domestic jobs to emerging markets, the ethical issues surrounding life and choice, and the need for a secure and economical supply of energy. While each of these issues is indeed important and deserves our national attention, none of them touches our society in so many ways as the energy issue.

The energy intensity of our economy, the mix and geographic distribution of fuels that we use, and the by-products of their use, all profoundly impact our daily lives. With the possible exception of the "price of money" (i.e., interest rates set by the Federal Reserve Bank), no single price affects the U.S. economy as much as the price of crude oil. Our dependence on natural resources located in politically unstable countries represents a potential threat to our national security, and our government spends a vast number of our tax dollars to reduce this risk. Fossil fuels such as petroleum, coal, and natural gas produce carbon dioxide (CO_2) when burned, which is widely thought to contribute to global climate change. Moreover, trace elements in these fossil fuels, such as sulfur in petroleum and mercury in coal are released into the atmosphere as pollutants. Taken in total, these influences may make energy supply the most pressing issue of our time.

Why is This Book Needed?

Given the volume of information available on energy issues, you might reasonably ask why this book is needed. The first reason is that the amount of publicly available information can be overwhelming. A Google™ search in mid-2006 on the exact phrase "U.S. Energy Policy" yields approximately 194,000 hits. Moreover, the official statement of U.S. energy policy is 170 pages long. This flood of information can be difficult to navigate for someone seeking a basic overview. The second reason is that opinions about energy policy tend to be strongly coupled to political views. I have carefully attempted to present you with concise information that should allow you to form your own opinions, free of personal bias. The third, and final, reason is that discussions of energy issues involve some degree of technical complexity. This book attempts to present these technical issues in a straightforward, digestible fashion. My hope is that when you have finished this book, you will have formed clear opinions based on the intersection of your own personal values and the facts presented here, and that you will assert these opinions in our democratic system to bring about positive change.

Chapter 1: Big-Picture Overview of America's Energy Usage

"Maximizing Energy Efficiency and Renewable Energy is the domestic epicenter in the War on Terror..."

-Alexander Karsner, Assistant Secretary for Energy Efficiency and Renewable Energy

Total Energy Consumption

Because the U.S. is such a large nation, statistics about its population and economy tend to involve huge numbers that are difficult to comprehend. Therefore, let's try to develop an overview of our energy consumption in an understandable context.

Figure 1 shows forecasted trends in energy consumption and production in the U.S.[4] The difference between the two, the "shortfall", is the amount of energy that we must import from other countries. From the graph, 2006 energy consumption in the U.S. will be just over 100 quadrillion BTUs. Your household energy bill probably does not state consumption in quadrillions of BTUs (British Thermal Units), so let's try to make sense of this number.

As a reference, one gallon of gasoline releases about 116,000 BTUs when it is burned. Furthermore, the current population of the U.S. is approximately 298 million people[5]. **So, on average, each man, woman, and child in the country will use an amount of energy <u>equivalent</u> to about 3,000 gallons of gasoline every year** – although our <u>actual</u> national energy supply comes from a mix of fuels including petroleum, coal, nuclear fuel, etc.

Global Context

Our national energy consumption is partially a result of the choices we make as individuals, but it is also related to the overall health of our economy. Generally, the more economic growth we experience (measured by "gross domestic product", or GDP, an indicator of the quantity of goods and services we produce), the more energy we consume. Therefore, one way to judge the energy efficiency of economies is to compare them on the basis of how much energy they consume to produce each dollar of

Forecasted U.S. Energy Consumption and Production

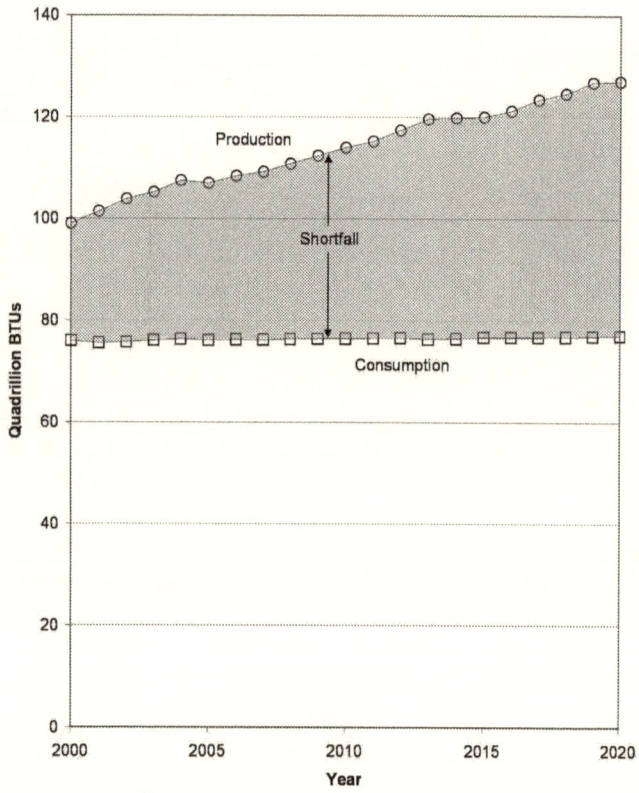

Figure 1 – Forecasted U.S. Energy Consumption and Production

economic output. This is sometimes referred to as the "energy intensity" of an economy. **Figure 2** provides such a comparison[6].

The graph shows GDP per capita on the vertical axis, which represents how much each citizen, on average, contributes to the various nations' economies. The horizontal axis shows energy efficiency as GDP per Million BTU, which measures how much economic value is squeezed out of each unit of energy. The ideal situation would be an economy that is <u>both</u> highly productive (towards the top of the graph) and highly energy efficient (towards the right of the graph). As you can see, the upper right box of the graph is empty, indicating that there is plenty of room for improvement. Compared to other countries, the U.S. has the most productive economy, but is relatively energy inefficient.

Because the nations shown in **Figure 2** have vastly different characteristics (for example, China's population is 1.3 billion, while Sweden's population is 9 million – a factor of 100 difference), a comparison of the total energy consumption per country provides additional insight. **Figure 3** shows this comparison[7].

Clearly, the U.S. is far and away the biggest consumer of energy in the world, but China's growing consumption of energy, driven by its emergence as a global economic power coupled with the sheer size of its population, is becoming a major influence in energy markets.

Energy Use by Sector

We noted earlier that the U.S. economy consumes just over 100 quadrillion BTUs annually, or the energy equivalent of roughly 3,000 gallons of gasoline for every man, woman, and child in the nation. **Figure 4** shows how this energy is consumed[8].

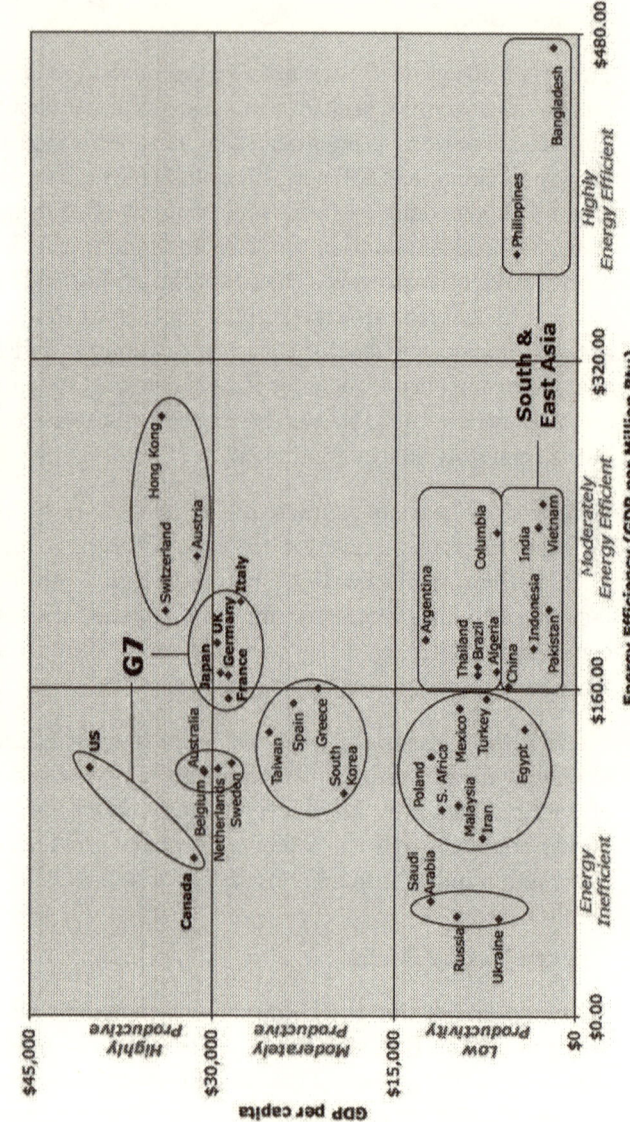

Figure 2 – Energy Intensity of Various National Economies

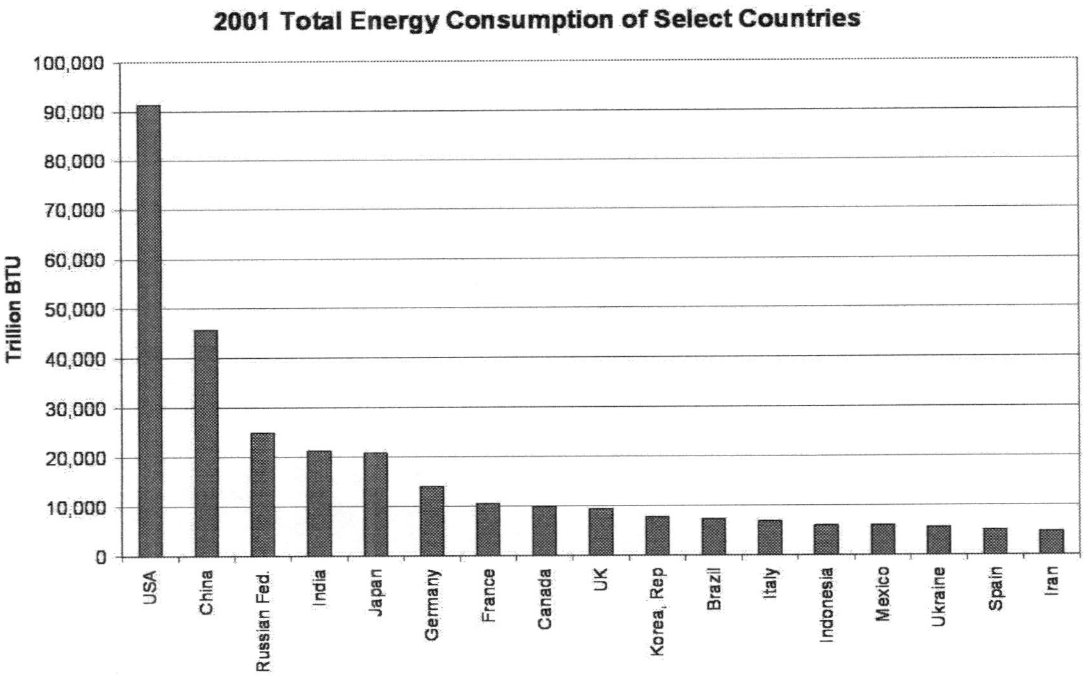

2001 Total Energy Consumption of Select Countries

Figure 3 – 2001 Total Energy Consumption of Select Countries

As a very simple illustration, the energy used to fabricate and assemble the car you may drive to the grocery store appears in the "industrial" sector; the fuel you consume while driving there is part of "transportation"; the electricity the grocer uses to refrigerate the food you buy appears in the commercial sector; and the fuel that your appliances use while cooking dinner in your kitchen qualify as "residential" usage.

Mix of Fuels

The 100 quadrillion BTUs of energy consumed by the U.S. annually are generated from a variety of fuels. These fuels generally fall into three categories: fossil fuels (such as coal, petroleum, and natural gas), nuclear fuel, and renewable sources, such as solar power, hydro-electric power, etc. **Figure 5** shows the total U.S. energy consumption by fuel source[9].

Fossil fuels are clearly still the dominant energy source, making up 86% of the total. Nuclear-based electric power has a small share at 8%, and renewable energy sources are still very much in their infancy, making up only 6% of the total.

Details on Petroleum

Since petroleum is by far the most important fuel used in the U.S. economy, and the price of oil is near an all-time high, you may find some additional detail on the supply and use of petroleum informative. **Figure 6** shows a "material balance" on petroleum in the U.S. – where it comes from, how it is processed, and where it is used[10].

For example, the graph shows that an average of 5.43 million barrels of crude oil was produced in the U.S. every day during 2004, while 10.04 million barrels were imported. Therefore, about 35% of U.S. crude-oil supply was domestically produced.

2005 U.S. Total Energy Consumption by Sector (Trillion BTUs)

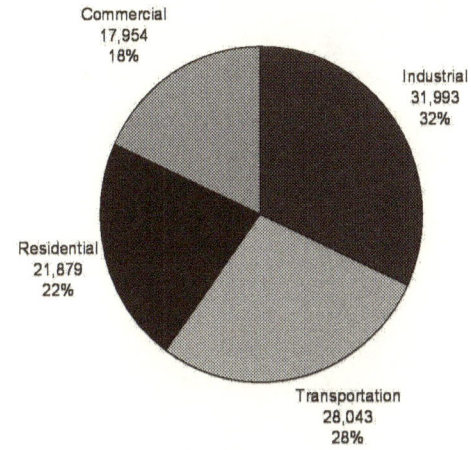

Figure 4– U.S. Total Energy Consumption by Sector

2005 U.S. Total Energy Consumption by Fuel (Trillion BTUs)

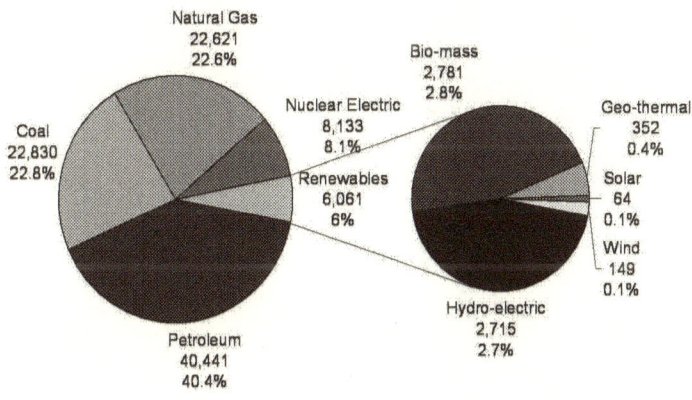

Figure 5 – 2005 U.S. Total Energy Consumption by Fuel Type

9

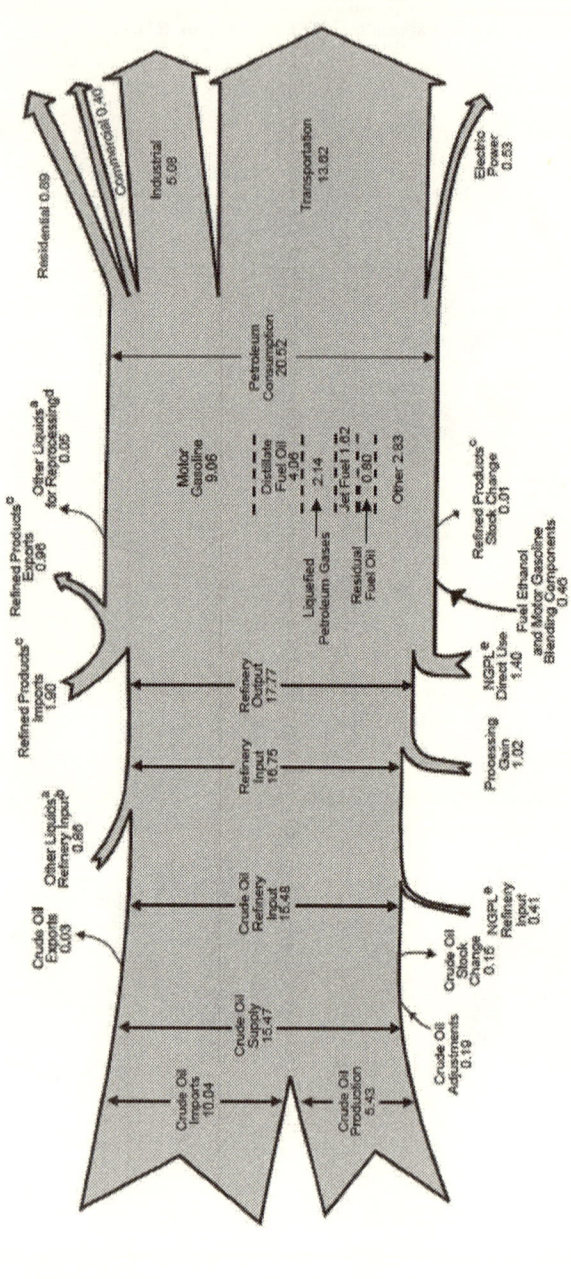

Figure 6 – U.S. Petroleum Flow (Millions of Barrels per Day), 2004

[a] Unfinished oils (net), other hydrocarbons, hydrogen, and oxygenates.
[b] Adjustments (-0.04), net imports (0.90), stock change (-0.05), and reprocessing (0.05).
[c] Finished petroleum products, liquefied petroleum gases, and pentanes plus.
[d] Unfinished oils requiring further refinery processing, and aviation blending components.

[e] Natural gas plant liquids.
Notes: • Data are preliminary. • Totals may not equal sum of components due to independent rounding.
Sources: Tables 5.1, 5.3, 5.5, 5.8, 6.11, 5.13a–5.13d, 5.16, and *Petroleum Supply Monthly*, February 2005, Table 3.

Crude Oil Imports 10.04

Crude Oil Production 5.43

Crude Oil Adjustments 0.19

Crude Oil Supply 15.47

Crude Oil Stock Change 0.15

NGPL[e] Refinery Input 0.41

Crude Oil Exports 0.03

Other Liquids[a] Refinery Input 0.86

Crude Oil Refinery Input 15.48

Refinery Input 16.75

Processing Gain 1.02

NGPL[e] Direct Use 1.40

Refinery Output 17.77

Refined Products[c] Imports 1.90

Refined Products[c] Exports 0.96

Other Liquids[a] for Reprocessing[d] 0.05

Fuel Ethanol and Motor Gasoline Blending Components 0.40

Refined Products[c] Stock Change 0.01

Petroleum Consumption 20.52

Motor Gasoline 9.06
Distillate Fuel Oil 4.06
Liquefied Petroleum Gases 2.14
Jet Fuel 1.62
Residual Fuel Oil 0.90
Other 2.83

Residential 0.69
Commercial 0.40
Industrial 5.08
Transportation 13.82
Electric Power 0.53

10

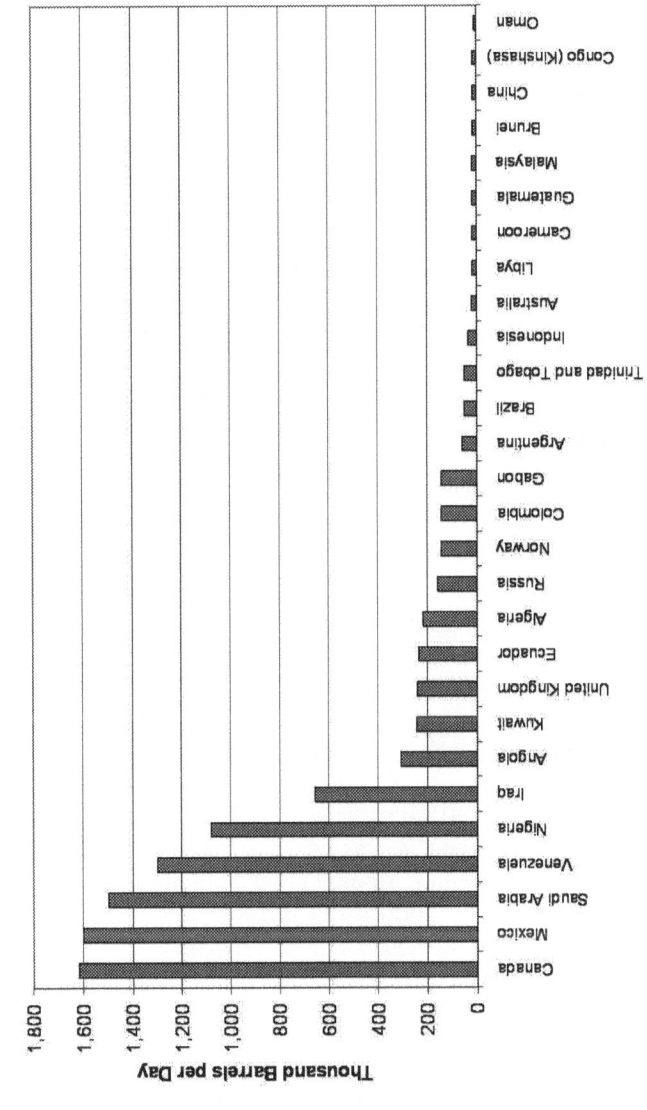

Figure 7 – 2004 U.S. Oil Imports by Country of Origin

The graph also shows that very few refined products were imported (1.90 million barrels per day – about 10% of the amount of oil refined within the U.S.). Furthermore, the refined petroleum products were used almost exclusively for transportation and industrial needs. Virtually none (8% of the total) went towards residential use, commercial use, and electric power generation.

The 10 million barrels of oil that the U.S. imported every day came from a variety of places. **Figure 7** shows an overview of the sources of U.S. oil imports[11]. You may be surprised to see that Canada and Mexico are numbers one and two on the list, respectively. Perhaps less surprisingly, Saudi Arabia, Iraq, Venezuela, and Kuwait are also near the top of the list.

Details on Coal

Figure 5 shows that coal is the second-most important fuel in the U.S. economy, just ahead of natural gas at 23% of total energy consumption. Coal imports are negligible - in 2005, over 97% of coal consumed in the U.S. was domestically produced[12]. Coal-based electricity generation is extremely cost effective, with rates of about $0.10 - $0.20 per kilowatt-hour (kWh). To put this in perspective, one kWh is enough energy to lift a weight of 800,000 pounds (equivalent to roughly 400 automobiles) by about three feet against the pull of gravity. Not bad for a dime – to quote one of my college physics professors, "Brother, that's the best bargain you've ever heard of!" A large coal-based power plant requires a delivery of 100 rail cars of coal every day, each car containing 100 tons of coal.

Details on Natural Gas

Natural gas is the third-most important fuel in the U.S. economy, representing 23% of all energy consumed. This section provides additional detail on its origins and consumption. **Figure 8** shows an overview of the

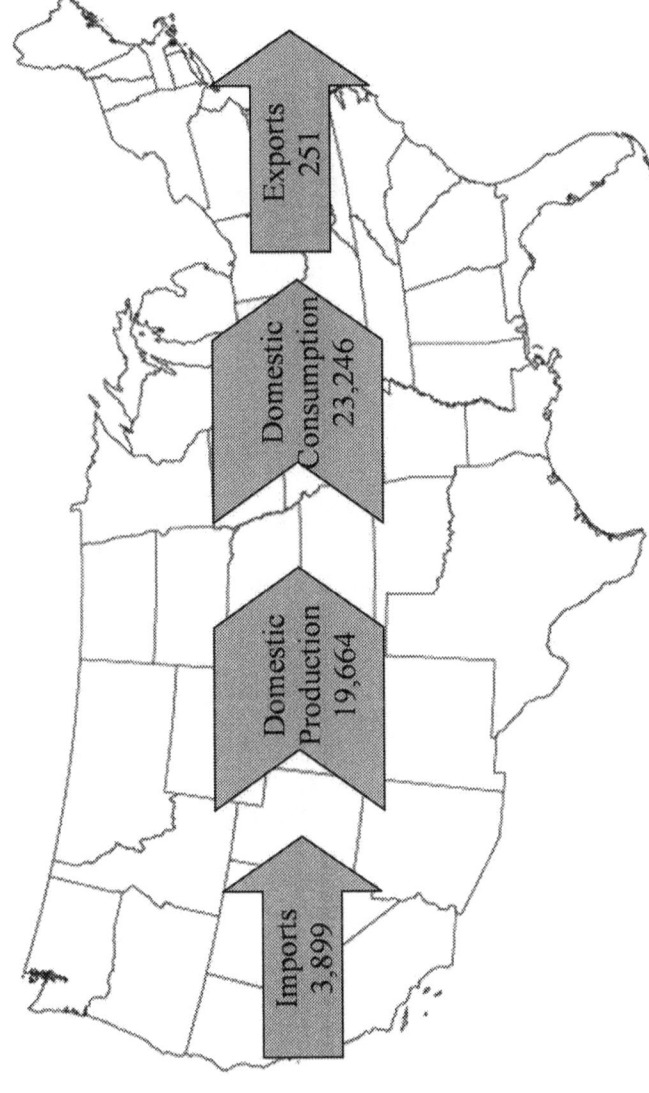

Exports
251

Domestic
Consumption
23,246

Domestic
Production
19,664

Imports
3,899

Figure 8 – U.S. Natural Gas Supply and Disposition, 2000 (Trillion BTUs)

supply and disposition of natural gas in the U.S. as of the year 2000 (note: production and imports do not exactly equal consumption and exports due to rounding)[13]. Approximately 17% of natural gas consumed in the U.S. was imported, while the rest was produced domestically. Of the 3,899 trillion BTUs of natural gas imports, 94% were pipeline imports from Canada and Mexico.

Details on Nuclear Electric Power

Figure 5 shows that nuclear fuel is the fourth-most important source of energy in the U.S. economy, representing 8% of total consumption. It is perhaps the most controversial energy source because of the juxtaposition of its compelling benefits, its potential for misuse, issues surrounding the storage of nuclear waste, and negative public perception caused by a small number of high-profile accidents.

Commercial nuclear power plants operate by generating heat via a nuclear fission reaction, using the heat to generate steam, and finally, using the steam to drive a turbine and generate electricity. The key attractive features of this process are that:

- There are essentially no emissions to the atmosphere during operation, except for clean water vapor from the cooling system.

- Nuclear fuel contains a tremendous amount of energy per pound. In fact, the fission of one pound of Uranium 235 (^{235}U) releases as much energy as the combustion of over 300,000 gallons of gasoline.

The disadvantages are:

- Spent nuclear fuel, as well as equipment that comes in direct contact with the fuel, remains radioactive (and hazardous) for thousands of years. This presents a tremendous engineering problem for safe storage.

- Both virgin and spent nuclear fuels have a high potential for destructive misuse, including use in nuclear weapons and so-called "dirty bombs". Nuclear weapons release the tremendous energy stored in the nuclear fuel via detonation, while dirty bombs use conventional explosives to disperse radioactive material in the atmosphere as a hazardous pollutant.

- Nuclear installations must be tightly guarded against potential terrorist attacks.

- Distinguishing peaceful nuclear energy programs from weapons programs can be extremely difficult. The international headlines regularly focus on this issue as, for example, Iran seeks to resume enrichment of uranium for what it claims are strictly peaceful purposes. The International Atomic Energy Agency and various western governments are seeking to block this step out of concern that Iran may be hiding a covert weapons program. In a Resolution adopted on February 4, 2006, the IAEA Board of Governors stated their "serious concerns about Iran's nuclear programme, and...that an extensive period of confidence-building is required from Iran"[14].

- Nuclear accidents, such as the Chernobyl disaster in Ukraine have dramatically influenced public perception of nuclear power for the worse. Chernobyl is widely regarded as the worst nuclear accident in history. The immediate impact included 56 deaths and the evacuation and resettlement of over 300,000 people[15]. Estimates of the long-term impact vary widely, from 9,000 eventual cancer deaths up to as many as 200,000[16]. After much study, the causes of the Chernobyl accident are well-understood and, to the extent possible, have been accounted for in the designs of newer nuclear reactors.

Furthermore, the world is being reminded of the potential long-term negative impact of nuclear accidents this year as engineers have been preparing to replace the hastily built "sarcophagus" that encloses the remains of the Chernobyl reactors. Cracks have developed in the concrete allowing water to pass the barrier and possibly spread contamination. A French consortium is managing the off-site construction of a huge (270m span, 100m height, 150m length) new movable sarcophagus (**Figure 9**), at a cost of approximately $768 million. It will be slid in place after completion in 2008.

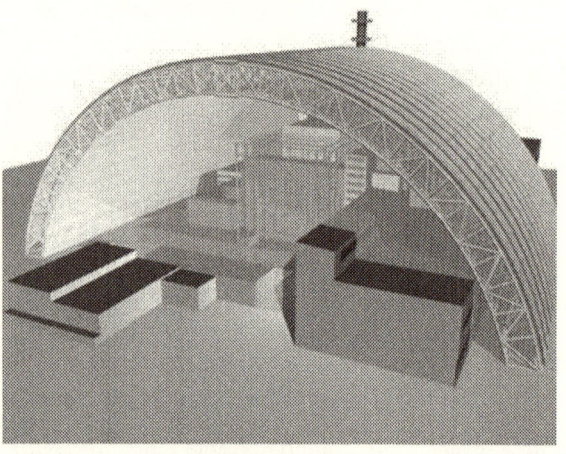

Figure 9 – Conceptual Rendering of New Chernobyl Sarcophagus

^{235}U is the only material found in nature that is capable of sustaining a nuclear chain (fission) reaction. Although other materials, such as Plutonium 239 (^{239}Pu) are also used in nuclear reactors as fuels, they are artificially produced. Uranium ore contains approximately 0.05% to 0.3% uranium oxide[17]. Raw ore is ground into fine particles and treated with a chemical solution to separate the uranium oxide from the other components. "Yellowcake", the uranium oxide powder that results from this process, is further processed into uranium hexafluoride, which is usually enriched for use as fuel. The equipment and techniques of enrichment are highly sophisticated, and governments and international agencies carefully monitor the flow of equipment and information to guard against nuclear proliferation.

Less than 1% of uranium found in nature is ^{235}U, while the remainder is ^{238}U, which is generally not suitable for use as fuel. Most reactors use uranium enriched to about 4% ^{235}U. Weapons-grade uranium is enriched to about 90% ^{235}U.

Perspective on Nuclear Risks

After reading about the risks of nuclear energy listed above, you may wonder why the technology hasn't been abandoned in favor of more benign sources such as solar power. This is a fair question, and to shed some light on the subject we should try to develop some perspective on risks.

If we were to survey the general public on whether they would be willing to allow the construction of a nuclear power plant in their hometown, you might expect a rather unenthusiastic response – even from those who, in principle, support the use of nuclear power. This is known as NIMBYism ("not in my back yard"). However, although this response seems natural and intuitive, it is not necessarily rational.

For example, consider a risk that most people are generally willing to accept in their everyday lives – say driving a car. For several decades now, the number of traffic-accident fatalities in the U.S. has averaged approximately 40,000 annually[18]. We think almost nothing of pulling into traffic every day, in spite of the fact that tens of thousands of us will lose our lives each year in doing so. By comparison, the infamous 1979 Three Mile Island incident was the most serious in the operating history of U.S. commercial nuclear power plants, even though it led to no deaths or injuries to plant workers or members of the nearby community[19]. Furthermore, the expected number of cancer illnesses caused by the small amount of radiation leakage from the plant is less than one case in the entire population[20].

In March, 2006 there were 103 nuclear power reactors operating in the U.S, one under construction, zero officially planned, and 13 proposed[21]. The compelling benefits of nuclear power, combined with the historically low risks, continue to create advocates for this technology. However, some critics argue that in a post-September 11th world, historical risks may not be relevant for establishing forward-looking policy.

Chapter 2: Consequences of America's Energy Usage

"In light of new evidence and taking into account the remaining uncertainties, most of the observed warming over the last 50 years is likely to have been due to the increase in greenhouse gas concentrations."

- Intergovernmental Panel on Climate Change

The previous section presented a big-picture overview of America's energy usage. By now you should have developed a feeling for how much energy we use as a nation, where it comes from, where it is consumed, and how our consumption compares to that of other nations. We now turn to the subject of how these characteristics of our national energy situation impact our daily lives.

National Security and Defense Spending

As shown in **Figure 5**, oil accounts for 40% of all energy consumption in the U.S, and more than 60% of this oil is imported. Much of the world's oil supplies are located in regions that are troubled by political instability and social unrest. **Table 1** shows estimates of proven global oil reserves by country[22]. In this case, the term "proven" means "estimated with reasonable certainty to be recoverable with present technology and prices". The risk of a supply interruption caused by political factors represents a national security threat to the U.S., to the extent that it would significantly disrupt our economy.

Furthermore, depending on your political views, you may believe that some portion of recent U.S. military activities (Persian Gulf War, 2003 invasion of Iraq, etc.) and homeland-security spending is attributable to a desire to secure a steady supply of oil from the Middle East. In fact, the present administration shares this view – a U.S. Department of Energy study stated that "the tragic events of September 11, 2001, remind every American of the danger of reliance on oil imports from politically unstable countries, some of which have opposing interests to those of the United States"[23]. Furthermore, a recent study by Columbia University economist (and Nobel Prize winner) Joseph Stiglitz and Harvard lecturer Linda Bilmes estimated that the cost of the current Iraq war could exceed USD $2 trillion, after consideration of factors such as ongoing health care costs for wounded or disabled troops[24]. This is a somewhat controversial claim, as

Stiglitz has been a vocal critic of the Bush administration. However, for purposes of illustration, this amount equates to approximately $6,700 for every man, woman, and child in the U.S. Some sources estimate the true cost of gasoline as approximately $10 per gallon because of such costs[25].

Table 1 – World's Largest Proven Oil Reserves by Country

Rank	Country	Proven Reserves (Billions of Barrels)
1	Saudi Arabia	262
2	Canada	179[2]
3	Iran	126
4	Iraq	115
5	Kuwait	102
6	United Arab Emirates	98
7	Venezuela	77
8	Russia	60
9	Libya	39
10	Nigeria	35

Climate Change

Again returning to **Figure 5**, we see that 86% of the total energy consumed in the U.S. is generated by the combustion of fossil fuels (petroleum, natural gas, and coal). This process releases carbon dioxide into the atmosphere, which scientists widely consider to be the primary cause of "global warming". Global warming is the term used to describe an observed increase in the average temperature of the Earth's atmosphere and oceans in recent decades. The scientific community generally agrees on a causal link between this trend and man-made greenhouse gas emissions. In 2001, the Intergovernmental Panel on Climate Change concluded that "in the light of new evidence and taking into account the remaining

[2] Includes Athabasca oil sands in Alberta.

uncertainties, most of the observed warming over the last 50 years is likely to have been due to the increase in greenhouse gas concentrations"[26]. However, the extent of climate change that we can expect in the future, the severity of the consequences, and what (if anything) should be done in response are hotly debated issues.

Evidence of Climate Change

The evidence commonly cited in support of a cause-and-effect relationship between man-made greenhouse gas emissions and global warming generally falls into three categories:

1. Observations of trends in global temperatures. **Figure 10** shows global average temperatures and predictions for the future based on several models[27]. Note that the scale of temperature change is on the order of a few degrees Celsius.

2. Corresponding observations of trends in atmospheric greenhouse gas (primarily carbon dioxide) concentrations. Modern-day concentrations can be measured by directly sampling the atmosphere, while measurements from distant history are based on ice core samples.

   Figure 11 shows two sets of atmospheric CO_2 data. The first set is based on ice cores from Vostok, Russia, and looks backwards hundreds of thousands of years[28]. These data clearly show that atmospheric CO_2 concentrations fluctuate over geologic time scales in a cyclical pattern. The second data set is based on measurements over the past 50 years at the NOAA Mauna Loa Observatory in Hawaii[29]. Combining the two data sets implies that modern-day atmospheric CO_2 concentrations are significantly higher than they have been at any time in the past 400,000 years.

3. Observations of changes in the earth's physical features, such as the retreat of glaciers. **Figure 12** shows an ex-

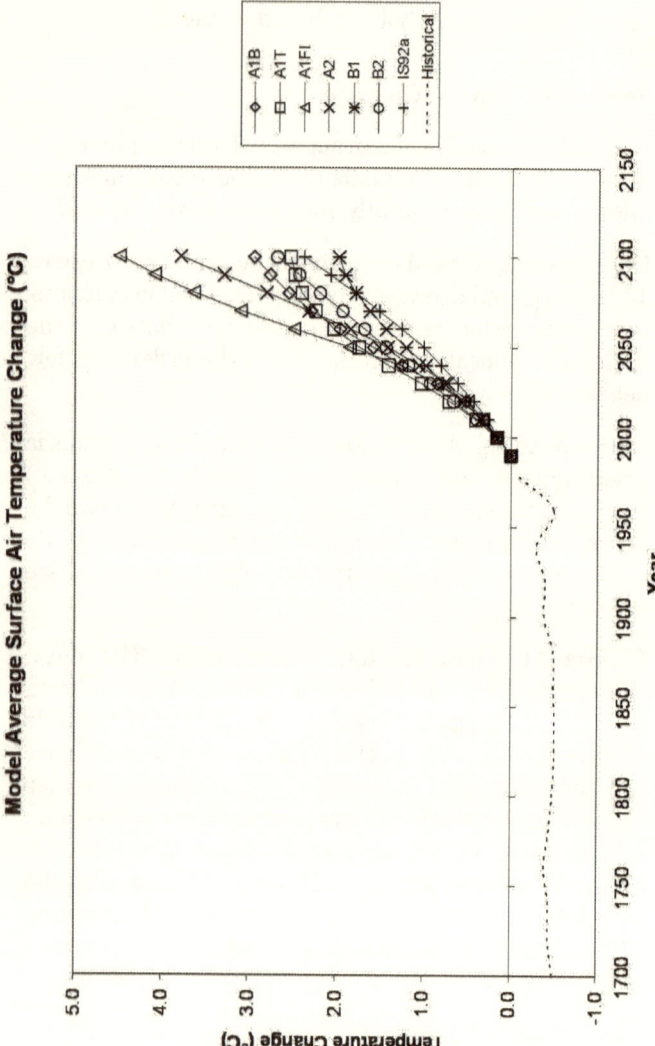

Figure 10 – Observed and Predicted Trend in Average Global Temperatures

ample of this in the Bhutan Himalaya[30]. According to USGS scientists, glaciers in the Himalaya are wasting at alarming and accelerating rates, as indicated by comparisons of satellite and historic data, and as shown by the widespread, rapid growth of lakes on the glacier surfaces. The researchers have found a strong correlation between increasing temperatures and glacier retreat[31].

Expected Impact of Climate Change

An increase in global temperatures could result in further changes such as:

1. An increase in global sea levels.

2. More extreme weather events, such as hurricanes, floods, and droughts occurring more frequently.

3. Retreat of glaciers and polar sea ice. **Figure 13** shows predicted decreases in sea ice thickness from 1950 – 2050 at the North Pole[32].

4. Changes in precipitation.

5. Pressure on the survival of sensitive species, possibly leading to extinction.

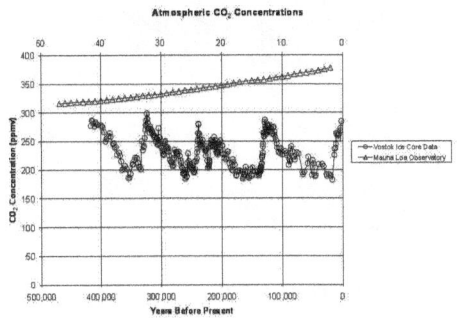

Figure 11 – Trend in Atmospheric Carbon Dioxide Concentration

Figure 12– Example of Glacier Retreat

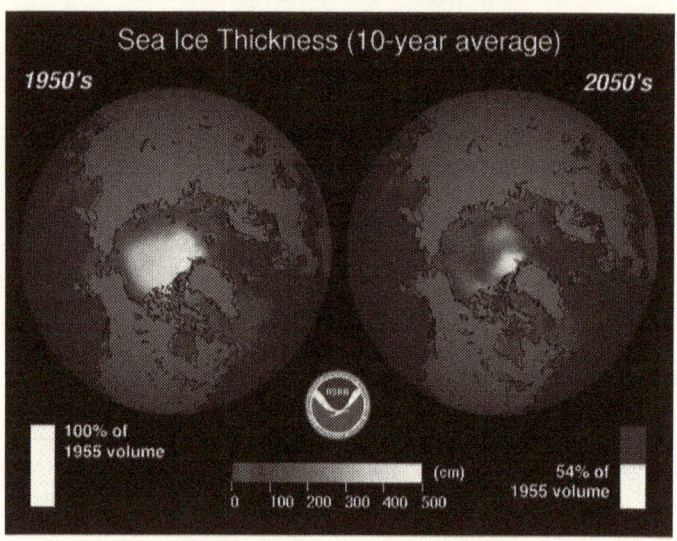

Figure 13 – Predicted Changes in Sea Ice Thickness

As discussed above, the magnitude of expected climate change and the severity of the consequences are widely contested, as are the costs that we as a society should bear to bring about change.

Strategies for Action

Proposed actions to fight global warming fall into one of four categories:

1. Reduction of energy use (conservation).

2. Shifting from carbon-based fuels to alternative fuels.

3. Removal of carbon dioxide (CO_2) from the atmosphere. Plant life is a natural sink for atmospheric CO_2 removal because plants use it is a raw material for photosynthesis. Artificial removal systems would (in theory) face the major disadvantage of having to treat giant volumes of atmospheric air to make an impact.

4. Prevention of carbon dioxide from entering the atmosphere and placing it in long-term storage (capture and sequestration). Options for sequestration include storage in unmineable coal seams, depleted oil and gas formations, and other natural geological structures. Geologic storage offers the added benefit of possibly enhancing the recovery of the lingering natural resources that remain in these formations – research shows that CO_2 injection can increase the recovery of oil from a reservoir by 10-15%[33]. Another option is injection into the ocean at great depths where the pressure keeps CO_2 in liquid form. Opponents of this approach raise concerns about raising the acidity of the ocean water.

Although the idea of storing huge quantities of CO_2 underground or in the sea may seem like an awkward "end-of-the-pipe" solution compared to avoiding emissions in the first place, it is important to realize that this process has likely been occurring naturally since plant life has existed on earth. The most commonly accepted theory on fossil fuel origins holds that they consist of

27

plant matter that was trapped beneath rock or mud and chemically altered over millennia by heat and pressure. If this is true, then the CO_2 released when we burn fossil fuels started in the atmosphere and was absorbed by these plants during photosynthesis. Ordinarily, plants decay after death, releasing carbon dioxide back into the atmosphere. However, under the scenario described above, the fossilization process locked the carbon into the earth's crust – acting as a carbon "sink" – until humans extracted it in modern times. In other words, by burning fossil fuels, we are releasing in a few short decades enormous quantities of CO_2 that took many millennia to deposit. Therefore, the idea of sequestering carbon is perhaps not as artificial as it initially seems.

The long-term stability and the cost-benefit characteristics of manually sequestering CO_2 are still under study.

Pollution

In this discussion, "pollution" means the unwanted release of substances to the air, soil, or water via impurities in fuels, combustion side reactions, or industrial accidents. By this definition, carbon dioxide emissions from the use of fossil fuels are not pollution, since CO_2 is a fundamental product of "perfect combustion"[3] using even the cleanest-burning fuels, such as natural gas.

Pollution from Petroleum

The combustion products of petroleum, especially from cars, trucks, and buses, contribute to air pollution in

---

[3] "Perfect combustion" is the theoretical ideal for carbon-based fuels, in which the only combustion products are carbon dioxide and water. "Imperfect combustion" generates carbon monoxide, soot, and other by-products as a result of non-ideal conditions.

densely populated areas. The exhaust from the engines in these vehicles consists not only of carbon dioxide and water vapor, but also volatile organic compounds (VOCs), carbon monoxide (CO), hydrocarbons, nitrogen oxides (NO_x), and particulate matter. These components react with one another in the presence of sunlight to form ozone and additional particulate matter, commonly known as "smog" (a portmanteau of "smoke" and "fog"). Smog, and ozone in particular, is an inhalation hazard that can aggravate asthma, worsen allergic reactions, irritate the respiratory tract, and reduce lung function. A 2004 study of 95 large urban communities in the United States (and published in the *Journal of the American Medical Association*) found a significant association between ozone levels and premature death[34].

Note that there is some confusion on the role that ozone plays in the atmosphere. In the upper atmosphere, ozone occurs naturally and protects life on earth by absorbing damaging ultra-violet radiation from the sun. Manmade chemicals, such as chlorofluorocarbons (CFCs), have reduced the amount of ozone in the upper atmosphere, resulting in the so-called "ozone hole". In the lower atmosphere, ozone is not naturally abundant. Rather, it forms from the reaction of VOCs, NO_x, CO, etc., and acts as an air pollutant. "Ozone action days", on which motorists are requested to refuel their cars after dark, are intended to limit VOC emissions from refueling when sunlight is particularly intense, with the goal of preventing the formation of ground-level ozone.

Pollution from Coal

Generally speaking, coal is one of the most impure fuels. Its impurities include trace quantities of mercury, arsenic, lead, chromium, aluminum, sodium, and potassium, as well as naturally-occurring radioactive metals, such as uranium and thorium. Coal also contains traces of sulfur, and the sulfur content is a key measure of the quality of coals.

The exhaust from coal combustion is called "stack gas", and it contains both gases and small particles of solids that are swept along with them. The gases include nitrogen, water vapor, and carbon dioxide, as well as small quantities of NO_x and SO_x, (nitrogen and sulfur oxides, which are contributors to acid rain) and other organic chemicals that result from imperfect combustion. Stack gas is treated prior to being released in order to capture the vast majority of solids (an example of so-called "end of the pipe" controls) and SO_x, and properly operating removal systems have efficiencies of approximately 99.5%[35]. Nevertheless, the small fraction of these solid pollutants that escape the treatment systems, as well as the gaseous pollutants, are the subject of much public discussion, since the amount of environmental harm done is difficult to quantify.

You might reasonably ask what harm is being done by this process, since (at least in the case of the solid-phase pollutants) the "impurities" are naturally occurring. During combustion, the volume of coal is reduced by over 85%, which increases the concentration of the substances originally in the coal. Although treatment systems retain most of the ash, heavy metals tend to concentrate on the tiny glass spheres that make up the bulk of the ash. These metals are released to the atmosphere with the escaping fly ash, at about 1.0% of the original amount, according to National Council on Radiation Protection and Measurements (NCRP) data[36].

The discussion on the naturally-occurring radioactive content of coal has several interesting features:

- Although the amount of radiation pollution caused by the combustion of coal is almost negligible compared to naturally-occurring "background radiation", it is approximately 100 times greater than that released by nuclear power plants[37]. **Figure 14** shows an estimate

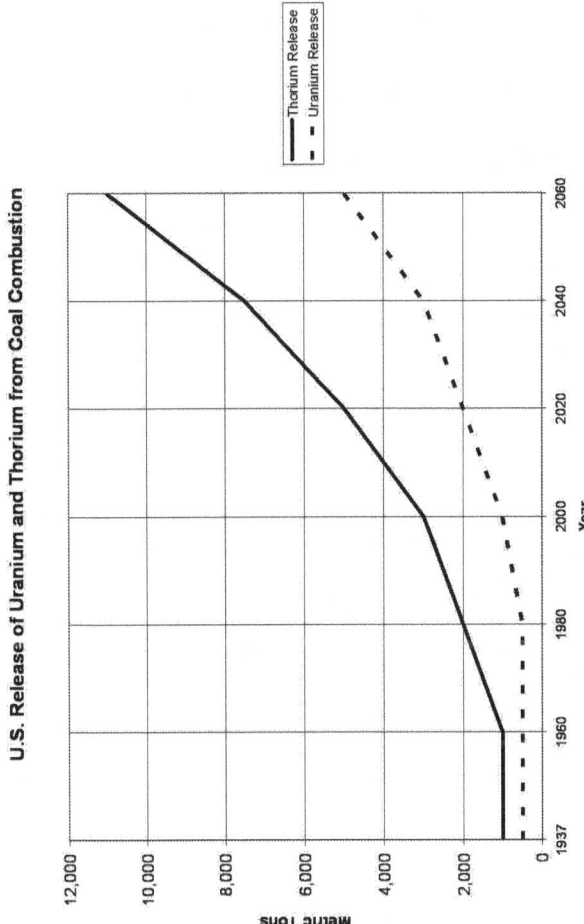

Figure 14 - Uranium and Thorium Release from Coal Combustion

of the total amount of uranium and thorium released via coal combustion.

- As mentioned earlier, electricity generation from coal combustion is extremely cost effective. Nuclear power plants suffer from a high burden of commissioning cost and extremely long construction lead time due to government regulation. However, there is no regulation of the radioactive emissions from coal power plants. Proponents of nuclear power argue that if these emissions were regulated, the economics of electricity generation would be shifted away from coal.

- Incredibly, the potential fuel value of radioactive materials emitted from coal combustion exceeds the fuel value of the coal itself[38]!

Economics

America's heavy reliance on oil (as discussed earlier, petroleum accounts for approximately 40% of America's energy usage, and over 60% of this is imported), has caused U.S. consumers a great deal of pain in recent months as oil prices have reached an all-time high. Many factors have contributed to the rapid price increases, including tensions in the Middle East, supply chain bottlenecks caused by Hurricane Katrina, and burgeoning demand from China. **Figure 15** shows oil price developments in recent years. Although political views about this issue may vary, one thing is clear – our dependence on oil leaves us susceptible to economic hardship.

Sustainability – When Will We Run Out?

Predictions of when the world's supply of fossil fuels will expire depend heavily on assumptions about the rate of discovery of new reserves, development of extraction

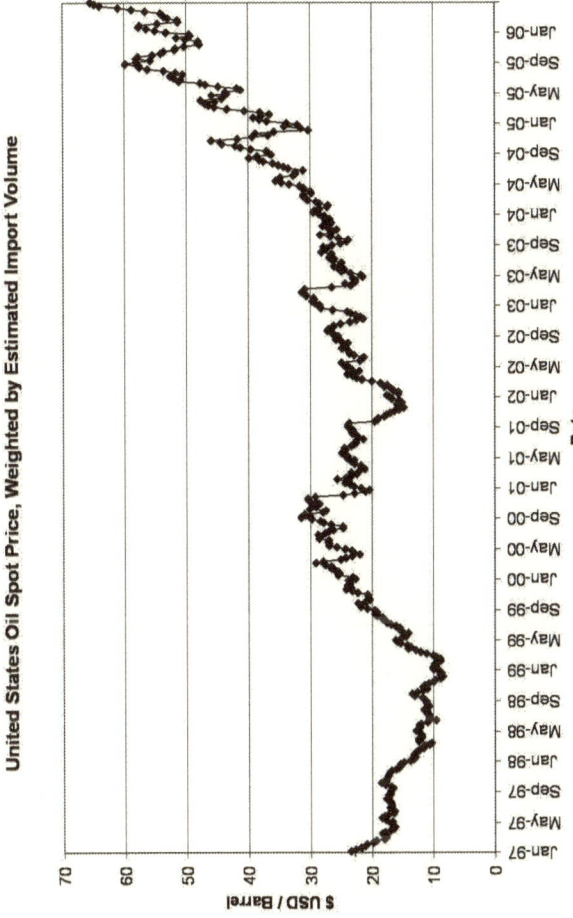

Figure 15 – Oil Price Trend

technology, and the adoption of alternative energy technologies. **Table 2** shows various scenarios[39],[40]. In the table, "BBL" refers to barrels (42 U.S. gallons), "CF" refers to cubic feet, and "ST" refers to short tons (2,000 lb).

Table 2 – Global Fossil Fuel Exhaustion Scenarios

	Oil	Natural Gas	Coal
Proven Global Reserves	1,300 billion BBL	6,200 trillion CF	1,000 billion ST
Current Global Rate of Consumption	30 billion BBL / yr	95 trillion CF / yr	5.4 billion ST
Date of Exhaustion Based on Current Reserves and Consumption	2049	2071	2191
Date of Exhaustion, Pessimistic	2075	2060	-
Date of Exhaustion, Optimistic	2200	2090	-

Chapter 3: Mechanism of Change: Market Forces or Government Policy?

"The two most important prices in the U.S. economy are the price of oil and the price of money (interest rates)."

-Anonymous

By now you should have a big-picture understanding of America's energy usage and the associated consequences for our society. Assuming you feel that the current situation leaves something to be desired, and that change is necessary, your thoughts may drift toward the best course of action to bring about this change. Our attention now turns to this subject.

Major options for driving change in energy usage fall into one of two categories:

1. Reliance on market forces.

   The U.S. has perhaps the freest market economy in the world. Proponents of free markets argue that they allocate scarce resources more efficiently than other systems such as central government planning. For example, in the U.S., companies are generally free to hire and fire workers "at will". Proponents argue that one advantage of this practice is that companies see less risk in hiring, and are therefore less reluctant to create new jobs. In contrast, some European countries impose onerous requirements on employers seeking to dismiss employees. Many believe that this offers protection for workers, but opponents argue that it generally causes higher unemployment because companies view hiring in these markets as a serious commitment. France offers a relevant example – unemployment is 10% within the overall population[41] (double the rate in the U.S.), 25% among young people, and 50% among the youth in poor suburbs[42]. In March, 2006, French Prime Minister Dominique de Villepin proposed reforms to the French employment laws including a probationary period during which new workers could be dismissed more easily than under the current law. The initiative failed – although de Villepin's intent was to create incentives for hiring, extended public protests caused his government to abandon the proposal and rethink the issue.

Free energy markets might efficiently allocate scarce resources in the following way. Assume that petroleum is the dominant source of energy in a market. If a supply shortage develops, consumers must reduce consumption or prices will increase. If prices rise, oil company profits will follow suit, attracting (in theory) new competitors to enter the oil industry. Eventually, the additional capacity created by new entrants will erode surplus profits towards zero. Alternatively, companies may invest in substitute energy technologies (let's say ethanol from corn) that are cheaper than gasoline or satisfy unfulfilled demand. In this way, the profit-seeking behavior of companies and individual citizens results in a constant "evolutionary pressure" towards the most cost-effective technologies.

This theory is elegant and works quite well in many markets. However, several aspects of the energy industry may limit the effectiveness of market forces in driving change. These include:

a. The consumer cannot always easily observe the true price of energy products. For example, in the case of gasoline, the customer generally thinks of the price as the number shown on the sign in front of the service station – currently (May 2006) averaging just under $3 per gallon in the U.S. However, as mentioned above, some sources estimate the true cost of gasoline as up to $10 per gallon because of hidden costs (e.g., military, homeland security, etc.) of securing a steady supply of middle-Eastern oil. Although this figure is politically contentious, it does illustrate the potential existence of hidden components of energy prices.

b.   The time scale of fluctuating energy prices is much shorter than the time required to create additional energy production capacity or change transportation infrastructure. For example, as mentioned in the introduction, President Bush stated in his 2006 State of the Union address that he seeks to commercialize cellulosic ethanol technology within six years. This is an aggressive schedule, but six years is effectively still a long time compared to the timescale of recent changes in gasoline prices (**Figure 15**). As such, consumers have relatively little short-term choice in responding to price increases. This is borne out by the observation that gasoline consumption has increased in spite of the recent tripling of price, making gasoline one of the few consumer goods without a negative price-demand correlation (how would you expect the consumption of coffee to change if the price increased from $8 to $24 per pound over the course of a few years?).

c.   Environmental responsibility is a type of "public good", and public goods are almost always under-funded. Examples of other public goods include public television and national parks. Consumers enjoy the programming on public TV and would be disappointed if it were no longer available, yet they are reluctant to donate, often because they feel that "others will do so". Similarly, the environmental costs of certain energy sources are undervalued by individual members of the public.

39

d. The energy industry has so much momentum that enormous investments are needed to develop and implement new technologies. This raises obstacles to progress, since even the most entrepreneurial of firms would be unlikely to attempt such a challenge alone.

e. Quarterly pressure from shareholders of public companies tends to narrow the focus of companies to the short term. For example, with oil prices at an all-time high, it would be hard to picture Exxon Mobil's shareholders demanding that their management team reinvest the company's record earnings ($25 billion in 2004) in unproven new technologies.

The combination of these factors may make a case for government policy as a mechanism for driving (or at least supporting) change in energy consumption.

2. Crafting government policy that creates incentives for, or mandates, change.

Government energy policy can take many forms, such as the following:

a. Tax credits for individual consumers to invest in favored technologies. For example, the federal government offers a tax credit of up to $3,400 to consumers who purchase a hybrid vehicle after 2005[43].

b. Subsidies to industry and academia for research and development of new energy technologies.

c. Regulation of disfavored energy technologies. For example, many state governments require emissions tests during the registration process for automobiles beyond a certain age. Furthermore, the federal government has phased out the use of leaded gasoline over time. Similarly, regulations limit emissions from coal-burning power plants.

One interesting approach is to combine government regulation with market forces in a sort of hybrid approach. Trading of emissions credits is perhaps the best example. In this system, the government establishes an overall limit for a certain type of emission – say, carbon dioxide. Companies are then given an individual emissions limit based on their type of business and the overall limit. However, companies can then buy and sell emissions credits from / to each other to optimize their own situations. A company that already outperforms the government requirement can sell credits to another company that doesn't have funds available to invest in pollution-control technology. In this way, the overall emissions requirement is met, but the individual members of the community decide on the best way to achieve it.

Chapter 4: Improvement of Traditional Energy Sources

"Man is the animal that intends to shoot himself out into interplanetary space, after having given up on the problem of an efficient way to get himself five miles to work and back each day."

- Bill Vaughan

One straightforward approach to improving the energy situation in the United States is to increase the effectiveness of traditional sources of energy. This section presents an overview of such opportunities.

Petroleum

As previously discussed, petroleum is the most important fuel in the U.S. economy, representing 40% of total energy consumption. Accordingly, improvements in the efficiency with which we use petroleum could strongly impact our overall energy usage. Conservation is one attractive approach, i.e., using less fuel to accomplish the same amount of work. Several well-known options exist, including improving the fuel economy of vehicles, carpooling, and developing an improved mass-transit infrastructure.

One common measure of fuel economy is the U.S. government's Corporate Average Fuel Economy (CAFE) standard. CAFE specifies the average fuel economy that each auto manufacturer's fleet must achieve in order to avoid fines[4]. This requirement increased throughout the 1970s and 1980s before leveling out (**Figure 16**)[44]. Proponents of raising the CAFE standards argue that the number has remained stagnant for over 15 years, while new technologies such as gas/electric hybrid drives make higher fuel economies achievable. They further argue that erstwhile commitments by car manufacturers to develop electric cars (which have since been abandoned) were merely attempts to avoid increases in CAFE requirements.

---

[4] If the average fuel economy of a manufacturer's annual car or truck production falls short of the CAFE standard, the penalty is $5.50 per 0.1 mpg under the standard, multiplied by the manufacturer's total production for the U.S. domestic market.

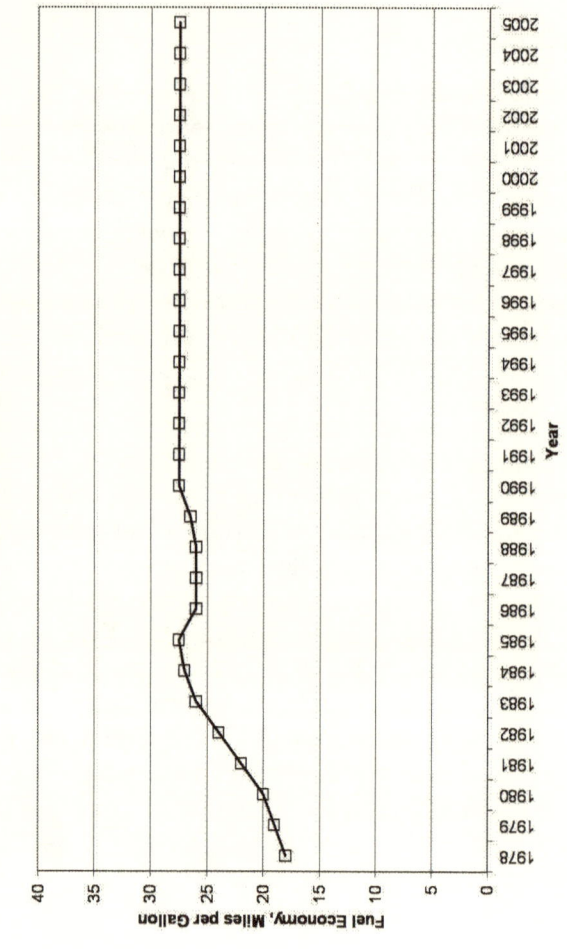

Figure 16 – Trend in CAFE Standard

Some opponents of increasing fuel economy requirements point out that consumer preferences have recently shifted towards less-efficient sport-utility vehicles and trucks, and that incentives and penalties belong at the consumer level, rather than the manufacturer level.

In 2004, Americans traveled 4.8 trillion passenger-miles on the highway in cars, trucks, and buses (one passenger traveling one mile is a passenger-mile)[45]. This is a proxy for the total amount of highway transportation "work" that must be done throughout the year. Also in 2004, American vehicles traveled 3.0 trillion miles, using 170 billion gallons of gasoline, diesel, and other motor fuels[46]. From these statistics, we can see that the average number of passengers per vehicle was only 1.6 (4.8/3.0) and the average fuel economy was 17.6 miles/gallon. Anyone who owns a car knows that adding a passenger to the vehicle has an almost negligible impact on fuel economy – the great majority of fuel is spent moving the weight of the vehicle, not the passenger(s). Let's consider the impact of increasing the passenger density from 1.6 to 2.0 passengers per vehicle via carpooling, assuming that fuel economy stays constant[5]. Doing so would mean accomplishing 4.8 trillion passenger-miles with only 2.4 trillion vehicle-miles. At a fuel economy of 17.6 miles/gallon, this small change results in an annual savings of 34 billion gallons of motor fuel (20% of the total annual consumption)!

The idea behind developing an improved mass-transit infrastructure is fundamentally the same – reducing traffic congestion and improving fuel economy by increasing passenger density. **Table 3** shows the

---

[5] Reduced traffic congestion and the corresponding reduction in wasted fuel during idling would likely offset any decreases in fuel economy due to the added weight of passengers.

percentage of commuters in select U.S. cities who use public transportation[47]. For perspective, consider that New York City ranks 49th in the world in terms of passengers per line-mile of railway[48].

Table 3 – Public Transportation Ridership in Select U.S. Cities

City	Percentage of Commuters Indicating Use of Public Transportation
New York, NY	54.4%
Washington, D.C.	34.5%
Boston, MA	33.1%
Chicago, IL	26.7%
Philadelphia, PA	25.9%
Seattle, WA	18.4%
Atlanta, GA	15.6%
Miami, FL	11.6%
Los Angeles, CA	10.6%
Detroit, MI	8.8%

Another approach to relieving the strain on the U.S. oil economy is to address supply constraints. Leading proposals include harvesting oil sands in Canada and drilling for oil in the Arctic National Wildlife Refuge (ANWR) in Alaska (which was first proposed during the Carter administration). Oil sands are laden with a tar-like substance that does not lend itself to conventional recovery. Instead, oil sands are generally strip-mined, which is an expensive process that only becomes attractive when oil prices are high.

Proponents of the ANWR option argue that:

- The proposed area for drilling is only 0.01% of the total land area in the refuge[49].

- The average estimate of technically recoverable oil in the proposed drilling zone is 7.7 billion barrels. This amount could fully supply the U.S. economy for a year, or provide 5% of our current usage for approximately 20 years[50].

- Estimates place the number of potential new jobs created at over 65,000[51].

- The reduced dependence on foreign oil would improve our national security posture.

Opponents argue that:

- Drilling would disrupt the lifestyle of Native Alaskan tribes.

- The proposed drilling area contains a "greater degree of ecological diversity than any other similar sized area of Alaska's north slope[52]."

- Previous oil-related accidents in Alaska highlight the potential for ecological destruction.

Coal

President Bush stated in his 2006 State of the Union Address (quoted at the beginning of this book) that "*we will invest more in zero-emission coal-fired plants.*" Such plants would theoretically represent a big improvement over the current technology, which generates significant emissions of carbon dioxide and various pollutants as previously discussed. The U.S. Department of Energy's "FutureGen" project will build a 275-megawatt demonstration plant that produces hydrogen and electricity while using carbon capture and storage to sequester emissions. The project will cost $1 billion and require over ten years to complete. It will be led by an industrial consortium representing the coal and power industries, with the project results being shared among all participants, and industry as a whole[53]. **Figure 17** shows a conceptual drawing of the FutureGen plant.

FutureGen will sequester carbon dioxide emissions at a rate of one million metric tons per year in order to stress test a representative portion of a geologic formation (with a capability up to two million tons per year). The site has yet to be selected from a short list of candidates.

Figure 17 – Conceptual Drawing of FutureGen Plant

Nuclear-Electric

Reprocessing of spent nuclear fuel is perhaps the most important near-term opportunity for improvement in nuclear power generation, while longer-term opportunities include the development of fundamentally new reactor concepts. As ^{235}U undergoes fission in a nuclear reactor, small quantities of "poisons" gradually accumulate over time. Poisons are natural products of fission that tend to slow down the reaction, eventually reaching the point of completely extinguishing it. Poisoning determines how often the spent fuel must be removed and replaced with fresh material.

Astonishingly, poisoned nuclear fuel still contains 99% of the initial amount of useful (fissionable) material[54]! Reprocessing technology, which is readily available, can separate and remove the poisons, allowing much more effective utilization of the fuel. Why then, don't we use reprocessing technology in the U.S.? The answer is that in the 1970's, President Carter issued an executive order rendering reprocessing illegal in the U.S. Reprocessing can also be used to develop weapons-grade nuclear fuel, and the administration's logic was that outlawing the process in the U.S. would send a strong signal against nuclear proliferation to other nations. Nevertheless, many nations including Great Britain, France, and Japan use reprocessing technology today.

Creation of long-term storage for nuclear waste is a second important improvement opportunity in the nuclear electric industry. Currently, nuclear power generators store waste on-site in "spent fuel pools", in which the spent fuel is submerged under water. The water provides cooling and radiation shielding over a period of a few years, during which the level of radioactivity decreases significantly. By 2014, the pools at all of the nuclear facilities in the U.S. will be full, and another storage solution will be required[55]. The Yucca Mountain facility in Nevada (**Figure 18**) [56] is the leading candidate for long-term storage, but the proposal is highly controversial.

In particular, the State of Nevada is opposed to the project. Polls show that most Nevadans distrust the US federal government based on the past history of nuclear bomb tests in their state, and feel that it cannot be trusted in current assertions that Yucca Mountain site will be

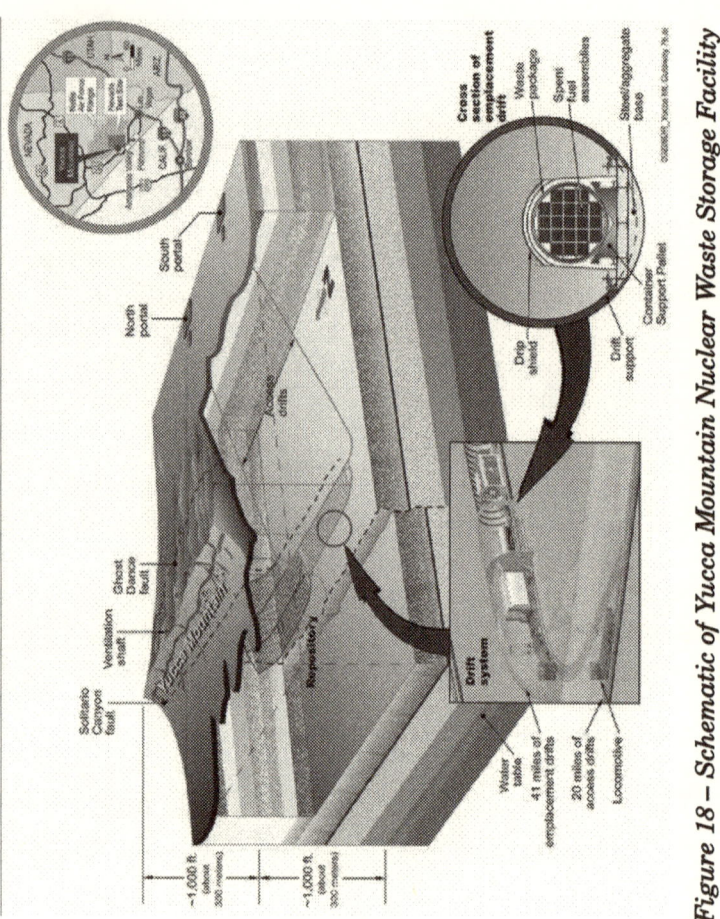

Figure 18 – Schematic of Yucca Mountain Nuclear Waste Storage Facility

safe[57]. A recent report by the U.S. Senate Committee on Environment and Public Works published the following conclusions[58]:

[Now is] a time to move forward – further delay is not an option.

- *Extensive studies consistently show Yucca Mountain to be a sound site for nuclear waste disposal.*

- *The cost of not moving forward is extremely high.*

- *Nuclear waste disposal capability is an environmental imperative.*

- *Nuclear waste disposal capability supports national security.*

- *Demand for new nuclear plants also demands disposal capability.*

Chapter 5: Development of Renewable Energy Sources

"The way out is through the door. Why is it that no one will use this method?"

- Confucius (Kung Fu Tzu)

Renewable energy sources are those that are replaced quickly (with respect to the rate of consumption) by natural processes. Fossil fuels do not meet this definition, but several emerging technologies do. Our attention now turns to these technologies.

A Step Back – Where Does Energy Come From?

Before we start our discussion of renewable energy, perhaps we should take one step back and talk about where energy comes from in the first place. The answer is straightforward – with the exceptions of nuclear and geothermal power[6], **all useful energy on earth originates from sunlight**. The fossil fuels we burn once consisted of plant matter that stored solar energy via photosynthesis. Wind power comes from temperature and pressure gradients caused by uneven heating from sunlight. Hydroelectric power owes its origin to the evaporation of water by sunlight and re-deposition at higher elevations via rain or snow. Even the energy you are using to read this book comes from sunlight, which was captured in a plant that you ate, or an animal that ate the plant, that you subsequently enjoyed for dinner. As we discuss options to provide energy for human activities going

---

[6] Stars, such as the sun, are giant nuclear fusion reactors. Fusion is a nuclear reaction in which smaller atoms are combined into larger ones, while fission splits larger atoms into smaller ones. Throughout their lifecycle, stars fuse hydrogen into helium, and then helium into heavier elements. Interestingly, ordinary stellar fusion cannot create elements heavier than iron, and in no case can stellar fusion create elements heavier than lead. All heavier elements, such as the uranium used in nuclear reactions are synthesized in supernovae, which are tremendous explosions that occur when stars larger than 1.44 times the mass of the sun (the Chandreskar limit) die out and collapse inwards.

forward, keep in the back of your mind that, in essence, for non-nuclear (and non-geothermal) energy options, our efforts amount to seeking effective ways to capture, store, and release the energy in sunlight.

Solar Power

The term "solar power" refers to the concept of harnessing the energy from the sun and applying it in useful ways. **Figure 5** shows that solar power currently accounts for only a tiny fraction, 0.1%, of total U.S. energy consumption. Nevertheless, it offers some very compelling advantages:

- It is free from reliance on foreign sources of energy, and therefore, strategically more secure than fossil fuels.

- It is sustainable, meaning that there are no concerns about when we will exhaust the supply of fuel.

- Solar power systems <u>operate</u> without any greenhouse gas emissions or pollution, although emissions during the <u>production process</u> for solar devices are an important consideration.

- Maintenance requirements are relatively low compared to other forms of power generation.

Disadvantages include the following:

- Sunlight is a relatively diffuse energy source. It strikes the top of the earth's atmosphere with a maximum intensity of about 1,300 watts per square meter (W/m²). Some of this light is reflected or absorbed by the atmosphere, and the portion that reaches the earth at sea level amounts to roughly 1,000 W/m². Furthermore, sunlight is (obviously) not available at night, so the average intensity over a 24-hour period is much lower than 1,000 W/m². **Figure 19** shows the

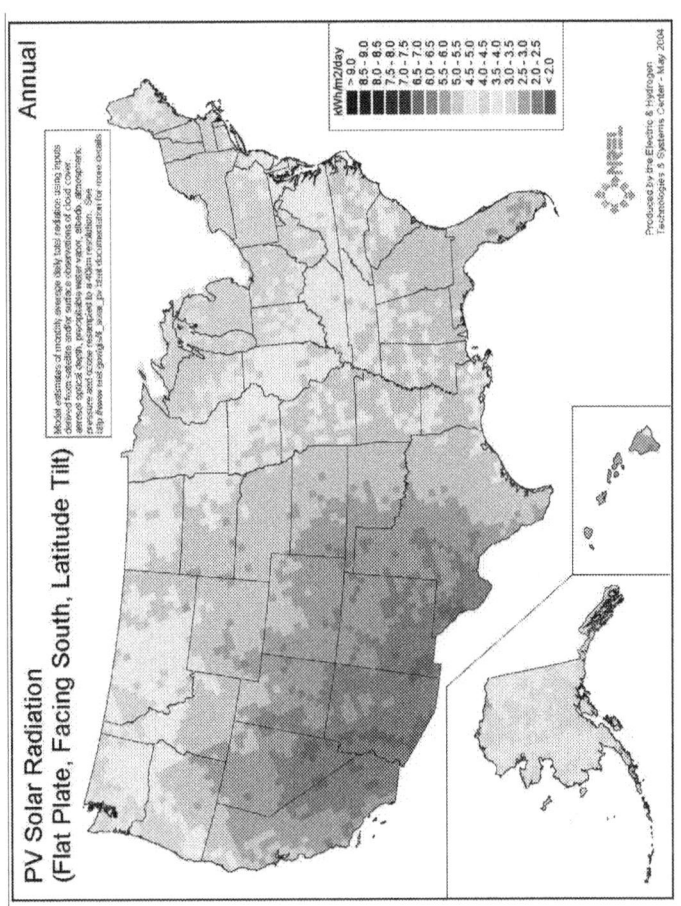

Figure 19 – Average Intensity of Solar Radiation in the U.S.

actual values for the United States. One thousand W/m², taken over a 12-hour period (daylight hours), is equivalent to 12 kWh/m². From the graph, you can see that even in the desert southwest of the U.S., the average value falls short of this theoretical value.

- Current commercial solar technology is not very efficient. For example, a typical solar panel that directly generates electricity (a "photovoltaic cell") converts into usable energy about 15% of the sunlight that strikes its surface. To put this in perspective, a large coal-fired power plant generates about 1 GW (one million kilowatts) of electricity at its peak capacity. A solar panel with 15% efficiency, located in the southwestern United States, would require a surface area of over 9 square miles to generate the same power.

- Sunlight intensity depends on the weather. On cloudy days, solar power generation is reduced significantly, making output somewhat unreliable.

- Sunlight is generally strongest in areas that are located far away from the energy requirements, resulting in high transmission costs.

Types of Solar Technologies

Solar power technologies fall into four important categories:

1. Systems that directly generate electricity from sunlight (photovoltaic, or "PV" systems).

   Commercial PV systems work based on the "photoelectric effect", which is the ability of certain materials to absorb the energy in sunlight and release it by liberating electrons that are normally tightly

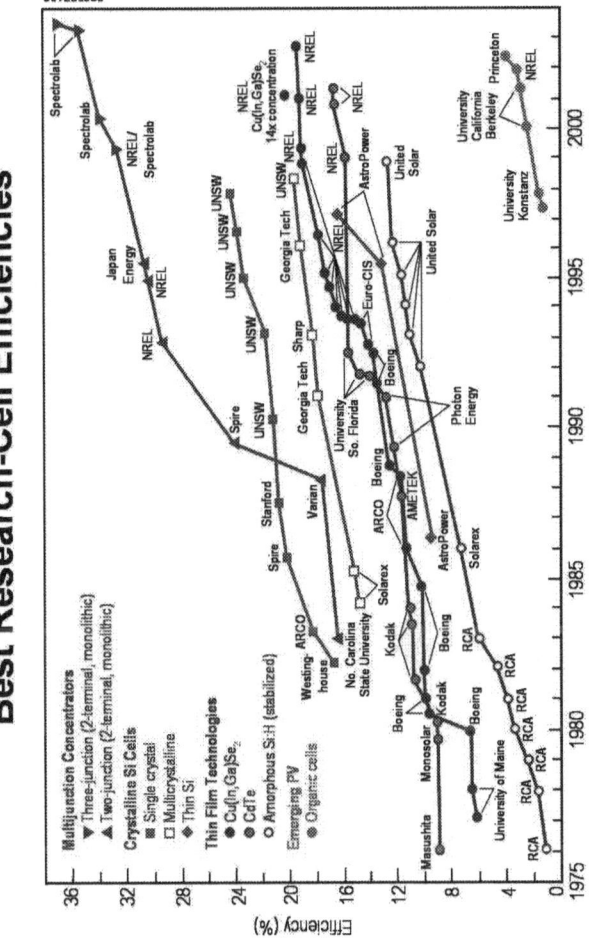

Figure 20 *Best PV-Cell Efficiencies Achieved in Laboratory Setting.*

61

bound to the atoms that comprise the material. The flow of these electrons constitutes a DC electric current, which can be channeled through a circuit to perform useful work.

The most commonly used materials in PV systems are semiconductors such as refined silicon. Silicon has the advantage of being readily available in nature (as silicon dioxide in sand), and relatively non-toxic. However, the current industrial production process for refined silicon operates at very high temperatures and produces about 1.5 parts carbon dioxide per part of refined silicon. More exotic semiconductors, such as gallium arsenide, absorb sunlight more efficiently than silicon (up to 39% efficiency compared to 15% for silicon), but they are much more costly and pose a health hazard due to their toxicity.

Figure 20 shows the trends in maximum solar panel efficiencies achieved in a laboratory setting.[59]

As of 2005, electricity generation costs for PV systems ranged from approximately $0.30/kWh in sunny climates to $0.60/kWh in temperate areas. Prevailing electricity prices from conventional sources are currently between approximately $0.05/kWh and 0.50 $/kWh worldwide.

Domestic PV systems are often connected in such a way that the homeowner can sell power back to the electricity grid when she has a surplus.

2. Systems that capture heat from sunlight and use it for heating, ventilation, or cooling purposes. Heating systems, which often provide domestic hot water, normally consist of a thermal collector, a fluid to transfer the heat from the collection area to the point of use, and a reservoir for storing the heat. A compact

solar heating system can save up to 4.5 metric tonnes of CO_2 emissions annually[60].

Solar cooling system technology is not yet mature, but is currently under development. The principle is to use solar hot water to compress a gas, which can later expand and cool the air through a heat exchanger, much like the operation of a conventional refrigerator.

3. Solar lighting systems, some of which use reflectors to concentrate sunlight and fiber-optic cables to channel it to the desired point of use.

4. Systems that capture heat from sunlight and use it for generating electricity, or so-called "solar thermal electric power plants". These systems use various means, such as parabolic mirrors, to focus sunlight on a heat transfer fluid such as oil or molten metal. The heat transfer fluid then passes through a heat exchanger to generate steam, which subsequently drives a turbine to create electricity. The 1,000-acre 330 MW SEGS system in Southern California is currently the largest solar thermal electric plant in the world[61].

One promising technology for storing solar energy is of particular interest to the auto industry. The idea is to use solar-generated electricity (either from PV or thermal electric plants) to split water into hydrogen and oxygen gas, in a process known as "electrolysis". The hydrogen gas, which is extremely flammable, can be burned or used in a fuel cell to power an engine (see section on Hydrogen). The primary advantage of using hydrogen as a fuel is that the only waste product is water vapor.

Hydrogen

Returning to President Bush's 2006 State of the Union Address, he stated that *"we will increase our research...in pollution-free cars that run on hydrogen"*. Hydrogen is intuitively appealing as a fuel for a few very compelling reasons:

- When burned (or chemically reacted in other ways) with pure oxygen[7], hydrogen creates only pure water as exhaust – that is, no carbon dioxide (greenhouse gases) or pollutants. Therefore, switching to hydrogen as the primary fuel for our economy could dramatically reduce the risk of global warming and air pollution.

- Hydrogen is the most abundant element in the universe, making up about 80% of all ordinary matter.

- Although the most economical process for producing hydrogen currently uses fossil fuel feedstock, in principle it is possible to generate hydrogen from water in a renewable way. This offers the tantalizing possibility of freeing ourselves from dependence on foreign oil and the worry of depleting finite stocks of fuels.

Nevertheless, several formidable technical challenges stand between us and a hydrogen-based economy. These challenges include:

- Production of hydrogen. Although hydrogen is the most abundant substance in the universe, it does not freely occur in its elemental form on earth. The current

---

[7] In practice, combustion with ordinary air is much cheaper than using purified oxygen. This can create small quantities of NO_x from reaction between the nitrogen and oxygen in air.

industrial processes for manufacturing hydrogen produces carbon-containing gases as byproducts, and burns natural gas to provide the required heat. This partially defeats the purpose of hydrogen-based energy – avoiding the emission of greenhouse gases. Furthermore, on a unit energy basis, the cost of hydrogen is still several times higher than that of gasoline[62].

Promising alternate technologies for hydrogen production include electrolysis (applying electricity to water to split it into hydrogen and oxygen – essentially the reverse of the combustion process) using electricity produced in a renewable way, for example from solar power; high-temperature electrolysis or thermochemical processes using nuclear power; and coal gasification (see the discussion about the "FutureGen" plant above).

- Storage of hydrogen. Pure hydrogen is extremely difficult to store. Today, storage is most often accomplished either by compression to approximately 10,000 psig, or by liquefaction, which involves cooling to extremely low temperatures – as low as -253°C (only 20 degrees above absolute zero!). Both of these processes are energy intensive. In fact the liquefaction process consumes about one-third of the energy value of the hydrogen[63]. Moreover, even in a liquefied state, hydrogen contains less than a fourth of the energy per unit volume of gasoline[64]. Finally, hydrogen molecules are so small and volatile that they are capable of slowly diffusing through even solid metal surfaces, and in doing so, they cause a phenomenon known as "hydrogen embrittlement" of metals.

Other hydrogen storage options currently under research include:

o   Chemically converting it to other, more manageable, compounds such as ammonia.

o   Adsorbing it onto the surface of solid metal hydrides[65].

o   Adsorbing it within carbon structures such as fullerenes or carbon nanotubes[66].

- Distribution of hydrogen. Over the course of many decades, the demand for conventional energy sources such as oil, natural gas, and electricity has resulted in the development of sophisticated and efficient distribution systems. In contrast, because there is essentially no market for hydrogen (other than captive use in the chemical industry), no such distribution network yet exists. Some automakers estimate that hydrogen would have to be available in at least thirty percent of the nation's fueling stations for a viable hydrogen-based transportation sector to emerge[67]. This presents somewhat of a chicken-and-egg problem: without a distribution system, there is little incentive to develop hydrogen energy applications, and without a market, there is little incentive to develop a distribution system.

In spite of these obstacles, the U.S. government is committed to a hydrogen-based economic future. **Figure 21** shows a projected timeline of the transition to a hydrogen economy[68], with the following key milestones:

- 2010 – introduction of government vehicles and bus fleets powered by hydrogen. Buses are attractive for this role because they can accommodate a large fuel tank and they tend to refuel in the same place every day (minimizing the need for distribution infrastructure).

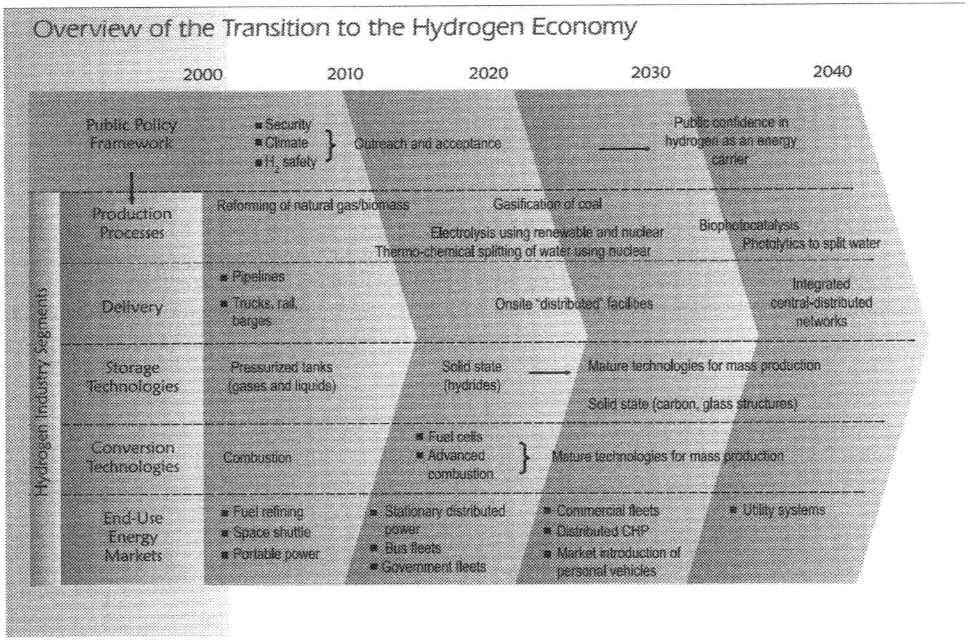

Overview of the Transition to the Hydrogen Economy

Hydrogen Industry Segments	2000	2010	2020	2030	2040
Public Policy Framework	■ Security ■ Climate ■ H₂ safety	Outreach and acceptance		Public confidence in hydrogen as an energy carrier	
Production Processes	Reforming of natural gas/biomass		Gasification of coal Electrolysis using renewable and nuclear Thermo-chemical splitting of water using nuclear		Biophotocatalysis Photolytics to split water
Delivery	■ Pipelines ■ Trucks, rail, barges		Onsite "distributed" facilities		Integrated central-distributed networks
Storage Technologies	Pressurized tanks (gases and liquids)		Solid state (hydrides)	Mature technologies for mass production Solid state (carbon, glass structures)	
Conversion Technologies	Combustion		■ Fuel cells ■ Advanced combustion	Mature technologies for mass production	
End-Use Energy Markets	■ Fuel refining ■ Space shuttle ■ Portable power		■ Stationary distributed power ■ Bus fleets ■ Government fleets	■ Commercial fleets ■ Distributed CHP ■ Market introduction of personal vehicles	■ Utility systems

Figure 21 – Hydrogen Economy Timeline

- 2020 – market introduction of hydrogen-powered personal vehicles.

- 2030 – advanced production, storage, and distribution technologies emerge, as well as applications such as utility and portable power.

Fuel Cells

A fuel cell is similar to a battery, in the sense that it converts chemical energy into electrical energy. However, unlike a battery, a fuel cell:

- is designed to be continuously fed with, and relieved of, streams of reactants and exhaust materials

- cannot store energy

Although there are many types of fuel cells, the "standard" cell uses hydrogen and oxygen (**Figure 22**)[69] as reactants to generate electricity, and produces water vapor as waste. Fuel cells can also use carbon-based fuels such as natural gas or methanol, which act as carriers of hydrogen. These types of fuel cells produce carbon dioxide and water exhaust.

Fuel cells play a key role in the overall strategy to develop a hydrogen economy. They represent an improved way, compared to combustion, to extract the potential energy in hydrogen. This improvement stems from the fact that fuel cells are not constrained by the same limits of thermodynamics that govern the operation of combustion engines. Current fuel cell efficiencies are in the 40-50 percent range, with up to 80 percent efficiency reported in combined heat and power applications[70].

Fuel cells are well suited for supplying steady power loads, but they do not perform well in applications where short bursts of power are needed. Because of this (and the

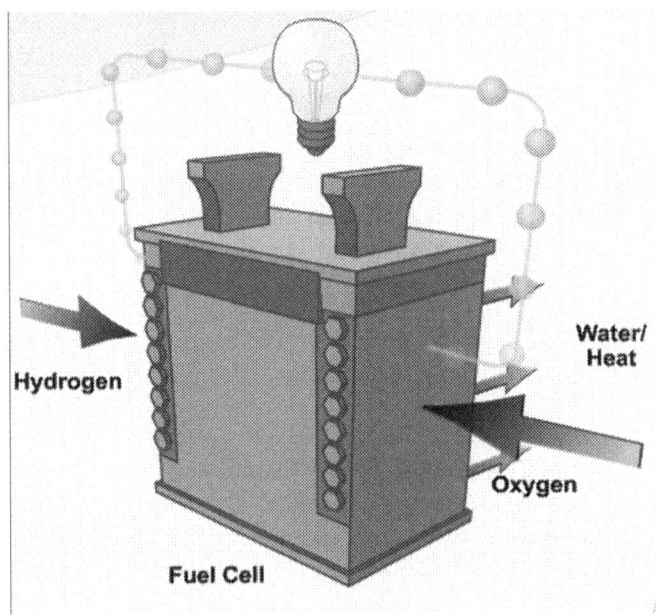

Figure 22 – Schematic of Hydrogen Fuel Cell

fact that they cannot store energy), automotive fuel cell applications will likely require a system that includes a battery as well. In such an arrangement, the battery provides short bursts of power, such as during acceleration, while the fuel cell supplies the power necessary for cruising and recharging the battery. The presence of a battery also creates the possibility to recapture some of the energy used during braking, as is currently done in some hybrid gas-electric engines.

A fuel cell operates in the following way:

- Hydrogen (or a hydrogen-containing chemical such as methanol) enters the fuel cell and touches the "anode", which is a porous surface, generally coated with a catalyst such as platinum.

- The platinum catalyst splits the hydrogen into electrons and protons. The protons flow through a membrane or solution called the "electrolyte", which allows protons to pass but is electrically insulating.

- The electrons cannot pass through the electrically insulating surface, and are forced to flow through an external circuit, creating the electrical current that performs useful work.

- Oxygen (or air) enters the fuel cell and touches the "cathode", which is similar in construction to the anode.

- The platinum catalyst on the cathode combines the oxygen with the protons and electrons emerging from the other side of the fuel cell, creating water and heat.

The main challenges surrounding fuel cells include:

- Reducing the cost of production. Most fuel cells use platinum as a catalyst to facilitate the reaction, which adds significantly to the cost. Using less platinum, or finding cheaper substitutes is central to reducing the cost. In 2002, typical fuel cells contained $1,000 of catalyst per kilowatt of electrical power generated [71]. The cost of power from an automotive internal combustion engine is about $25-35 per kilowatt, and the cost of fuel cells must fall below $50 per kilowatt to be competitive[72].

- The required durability of fuel cell systems has not yet been proven. Fuel cell power systems will be required to withstand automotive conditions, including a 5,000 hour lifespan (150,000 miles equivalent) and the ability to function over the full range of vehicle operating conditions (-40° to +40° C) [73].

- Managing the sensitive air input to, and heat and water outputs from, fuel cell systems.

- Reducing the size and weight of fuel cell systems to be suitable for use in automotive applications.

Ethanol

The term "biomass fuels" or "biofuels" collectively refers to the group of fuels derived from recently living organisms or their metabolic by-products. Bioethanol is one important example of a biomass fuel. Humans have produced ethanol, also known as "grain alcohol" or "ethyl alcohol", from biomass for millennia – winemaking is a classical example, in which yeast ferments the sugars in grapes to yield a beverage with 10-15% ethanol content. Ethanol is a flammable liquid at higher concentrations, making it especially interesting for use as motor fuel.

Interest in ethanol as a fuel originally developed during the oil embargo crisis of 1973, and has been rekindled with the tripling of oil prices from mid-2003 to early 2006 (see **Figure 15**). Returning again to President Bush's 2006 State of the Union Address, he stated that "*we must also change how we power our automobiles…we'll…fund additional research in cutting-edge methods of producing ethanol, not just from corn, but from wood chips and stalks, or switch grass. Our goal is to make this new kind of ethanol practical and competitive within six years.*"

The potential benefits of ethanol biofuel include:

- It is a renewable energy source, meaning that it can be replenished in a relatively short timeframe compared to the rate of consumption, and it consumes less fossil fuel energy in production than the energy content of the product.

- Although the production and combustion of ethanol both release CO_2 to the atmosphere, taken as a whole this is a carbon-neutral process. This means that it does not add to the total quantity of CO_2 in the atmosphere. This is true because the carbon content of the ethanol comes from carbon dioxide that the corn (or other crop) plant takes in from the atmosphere and converts to sugars via photosynthesis. Although the carbon in fossil fuels also likely came from photosynthesis, it has been sequestered in the ground for millennia. As we burn vast quantities of these fuels much faster than the regeneration process, the net effect is an increase in atmospheric CO_2 concentrations.

- The vast agricultural resources of the U.S. mean that ethanol can be produced domestically, reducing our dependence on foreign oil and improving our national security posture.

- Increasing demand for ethanol-producing crops should reduce the $16 billion in agricultural subsidies that U.S. taxpayers fund annually[74].

- Because ethanol is an oxygenated fuel, combustion engines running on ethanol produce much less carbon monoxide emissions than their fossil-fuel powered counterparts.

Key challenges for the development of an ethanol-based transportation sector include:

- Reducing the cost of production and distribution.

- Increasing the availability of "flex-fuel" vehicles, which can accept either E85 (85% ethanol, 15% gasoline) or conventional gasoline.

Figure 23 shows how the energy content of ethanol compares to other liquid fuels[75].

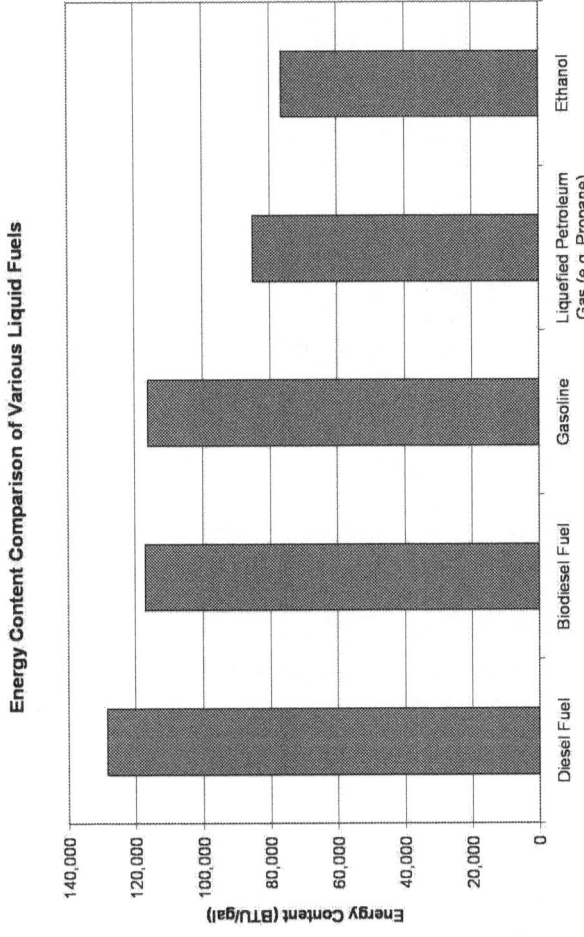

Figure 23 – Energy Content Comparison of Various Liquid Fuels

Methods of Production

Ethanol production from corn is currently the dominant biomass-based process. Production (by the dry-mill process) consists of the following major steps[76]:

1. A hammer mill breaks the corn kernel down into a coarse flour-like consistency.

2. The corn is cooked in water, and enzymes are added to convert starch to glucose (sugar).

3. Yeast ferments the sugary mixture, resulting in 12-15% ethanol on a volume basis. This material is known as "beer".

4. The beer is separated into liquids and solids.

5. The liquid is distilled to concentrate the ethanol to about 96%, while the solids are dried and re-used as, for example, animal feed.

6. Molecular sieves (which are essentially microscopic filters that are sized to allow water to pass but retain ethanol) remove water and increase the ethanol purity to greater than 99%. Low water content is critical to prevent separation problems when the ethanol is blended with gasoline.

Because this process is relatively mature, cost reduction efforts are focused on improving corn crop yields, reducing waste heat, increasing automation, etc. In parallel, the industry is also developing an ethanol production process based on a completely different feedstock – cellulose instead of corn – which is expected to result in much more significant cost savings than optimization of the corn process.

Cellulose is the primary structural component of green plants, and as such, is the most abundant form of biomass on earth. The major potential cost savings compared to corn-based production is the low cost of the feedstock. Waste materials, such as grass clippings, corn stalks, wood chips, and sugar cane bagasse can all be used as feedstock in a cellulosic ethanol process, as can low-cost plants grown specifically for this purpose, such as switchgrass, hybrid poplars, and willows[77].

The technology to produce ethanol from cellulose currently exists, but is not yet economically competitive with the corn-based process. Several different cellulose-based processes are being developed in parallel, with the primary difference being the way in which the biomass is broken down into sugars that can be fermented into ethanol:

- <u>Dilute</u> sulfuric acid process. The major drawback of this process is the tendency to produce large quantities of by-products[78].

- <u>Concentrated</u> sulfuric acid process. The major drawback of this process is the cost of recycling the acid[79].

- Enzyme process. The major drawback of this process is the current cost of the enzymes. Reducing the cost of this process is the most important cost-savings opportunity in biomass ethanol production.

Energy Balance Controversy

Some critics of fuel ethanol have claimed that ethanol production has a "negative energy balance", meaning that the production process consumes more energy than the resulting product contains[80]. Ethanol advocates claim that this analysis is politically biased, based on outdated information, and highly dependent on the choice of boundaries for the production process – i.e., how far upstream it extends. Let's take a closer look at this issue to see if we can develop some additional insights.

At first glance, the notion that we should only pursue an energy-related process if it yields more energy than must be invested in it seems logical and intuitive. However, further analysis shows that this is clearly not true. Consider, for example, a coal-fired power plant. Typical coal-fired plants achieve an energy conversion efficiency of about 38%[81]. This means that for each 100 BTU of heat we release by burning coal, only 38 BTU winds up as electricity – the remaining 62 BTU is lost as waste heat. Why would we engage in a process that only yields 38 BTU of useful energy for every 100 BTU of energy input? The answer is that consumers find it more convenient to use energy in the form of electricity delivered via the wires infrastructure than to receive deliveries of coal at their homes.

The same argument holds for the oil refining process. The BTU content of the product streams leaving a refinery equals the BTU content of the crude oil input stream, minus any yield losses. Overall, the process has a negative energy balance, since separating the oil into its components requires energy input and results in no energy gain. Again, why perform such a process? Because automobile engines run much better on gasoline than they do on crude oil – again, the decision is based on convenience and accessibility.

Returning to the case of ethanol, would a negative overall energy balance necessarily mean that it is a futile technology? As was the case in the coal and oil examples, the answer is "not necessarily". Ethanol is primarily intended as a substitute for oil – that is, as a liquid fuel that can be used in automobiles and similar applications. Accordingly, we should only categorically rule out the pursuit of the technology if it increases total oil consumption. Otherwise, the decision should be made on the basis of the relative cost of the technology and the net impact on fuel consumption from a strategic (e.g., national security) perspective.

In fact, the U.S. Department of Energy claims that the net energy balance for making fuel ethanol from corn, based on current technology, is 1.34[82]. This means that for every BTU invested in growing corn and turning it into ethanol, we receive 1.34 units of energy output.[8]

Biodiesel

The term "biodiesel" refers to fuels that are chemically similar to ordinary diesel fuel (and generally can be used in a standard diesel engine), but are made from agricultural or waste oils rather than petroleum. European biodiesel is most often made from rapeseed oil (a cousin of canola oil), while soybean oil is the most prominent feedstock in the U.S., primarily because of the established nature of the soybean industry in this country[83]. As a biomass fuel, biodiesel offers many of the same potential benefits as bioethanol, including:

- It is a renewable energy source.

- The combustion process is essentially carbon neutral. **Figure 24** depicts the carbon cycle for biodiesel fuel[84].

- Domestic production capability reduces our dependence on foreign oil and improves our national security posture.

---

[8] Like the coal combustion and oil refining examples, the corn feedstock contains more energy than the ethanol product – i.e., less than 100% is converted into useful energy. However, the lost energy originates from the sunlight that the corn plant converts into sugars. This energy is, in a sense, "free" since it is independent of the energy we must invest in growing the corn and converting it into ethanol.

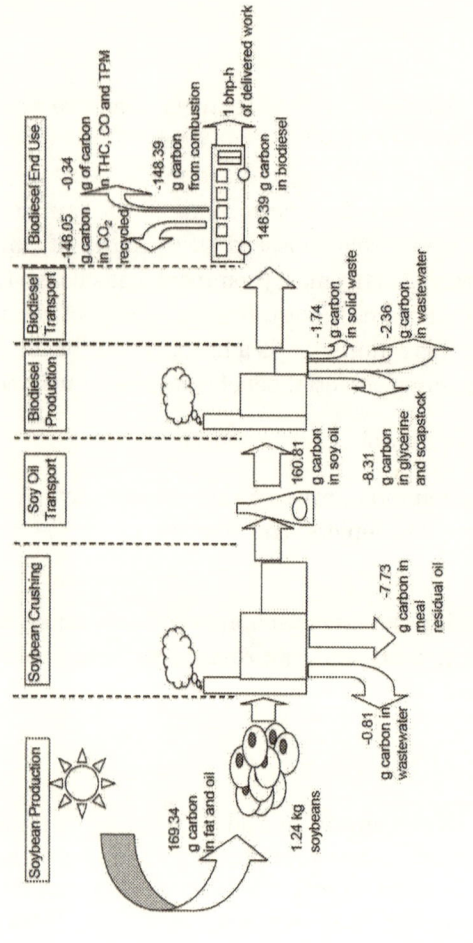

Figure 24 – Biodiesel Carbon Cycle

78

- Increasing demand for biodiesel-producing crops should reduce the $16 billion in agricultural subsidies that U.S. taxpayers fund annually[85].

Furthermore, biodiesel offers a higher volumetric energy density than ethanol. **Figure 23** shows this comparison. Finally, compared to petroleum diesel, biodiesel offers:

- Reduced emissions of particulate matter (32%), carbon monoxide (35%) and sulfur dioxide (8%) relative to petroleum diesel's life cycle. However this benefit is partially offset by increases in NO_x and hydrocarbon emissions (13.35% and 35%, respectively) [86].

- Low toxicity.

The key challenges associated with biodiesel include:

- Lowering the cost of production and distribution, and optimizing the yield from the feedstock. Although the existing infrastructure in the U.S. makes soybean oil a leading feedstock candidate, other crops (especially algae) are also promising, as shown in **Table 4**[87].

Table 4 – Biodiesel Yields of Various Crops

Crop	Potential Biodiesel Yield (Gallons per U.S. Acre per Year)
Soybean	40 – 50
Rapeseed	110 – 145
Mustard	140
Palm Oil	650
Algae	10,000 – 20,000

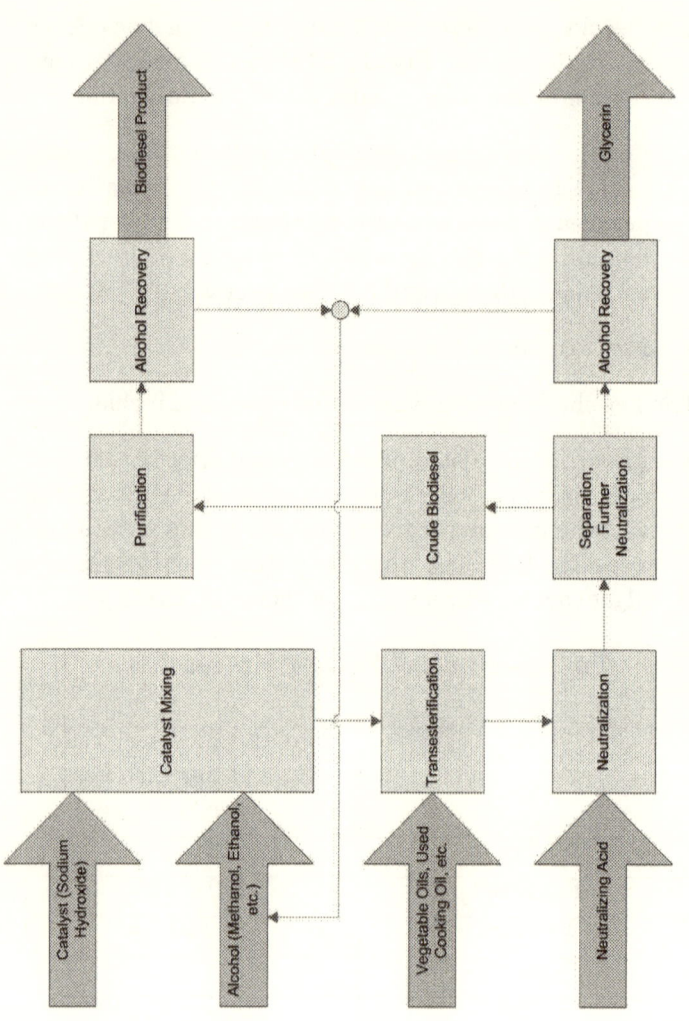

Figure 25 – Biodiesel Production Process

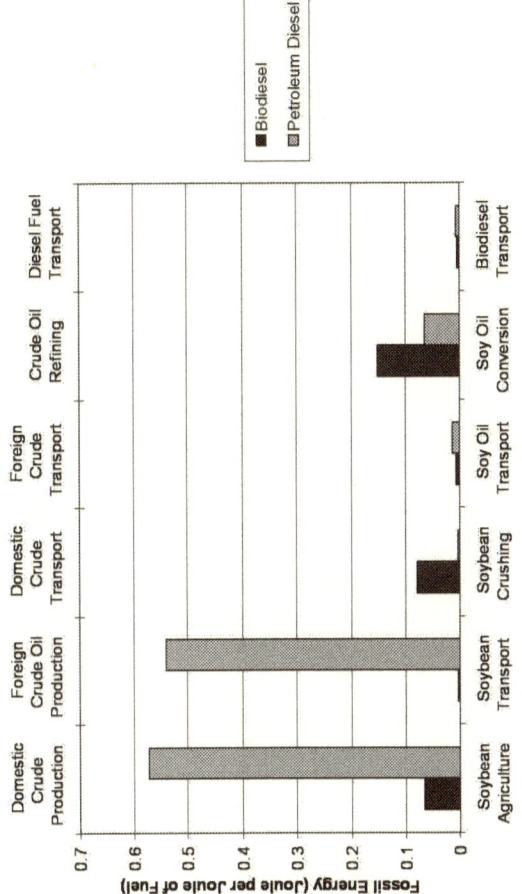

Figure 26 – Fossil Energy Requirements for Petroleum Diesel and Biodiesel Production

- Limiting the water content of the biodiesel. Biodiesel is "hydrophilic", meaning that it tends to attract water. Water is problematic in biodiesel for several reasons, including reduced heat of combustion (more smoke, harder starting, less power), corrosion of fuel system components, accelerated gelling of the fuel, and promotion of microbe growth which can clog the fuel system[88].

- Improving cold-flow properties. Biodiesel tends to gel around 4°C. This is most commonly addressed by blending with petroleum diesel[89].

Methods of Production

Biodiesel is created by chemically combining oils and alcohols in what is known as a "trans-esterification" reaction. Currently, the most-commonly used alcohol for this purpose is methanol, although ethanol or higher alcohols can be used as well. Methanol is produced from petroleum feedstock, while ethanol (as previously discussed) can be produced from renewable biomass. Biodiesel production creates glycerin as a useful by-product. **Figure 25** shows an overview of a typical production process[90].

Energy Balance

Biodiesel is renewable because the source crop can be quickly replenished and the process yields more energy content in the product fuel than it consumes in fossil energy during production. **Figure 26** compares biodiesel and petrodiesel in this respect[91]. Biodiesel consumes a total of 0.311 joules of fossil energy per joule of product energy, while petrodiesel consumes 1.299 joules of fossil energy per joule of product energy.

The energy balance shown above assumes that methanol (which is produced from petroleum feedstock) is the alcohol used to create biodiesel. If a biomass alcohol, such as ethanol, were used instead, the fossil energy requirements for biodiesel production would be significantly reduced.

Wind Energy

Humans have harnessed the energy of the wind for thousands of years – one classical example is the use of sails to power ships. Modern wind turbines, which are often arrayed in "wind farms" (**Figure 27**)[92], generate electricity from the rotation of their blades. Although the generation of electricity from wind power has grown rapidly in recent years, it still only represents a fraction of a percent of the total U.S. annual energy consumption (see **Figure 5**). Nevertheless, advocates of wind technology feel that it is poised to play a larger role in satisfying our national energy needs because of its many compelling advantages.

Figure 27 – Wind Farm Off of the Coast of Denmark

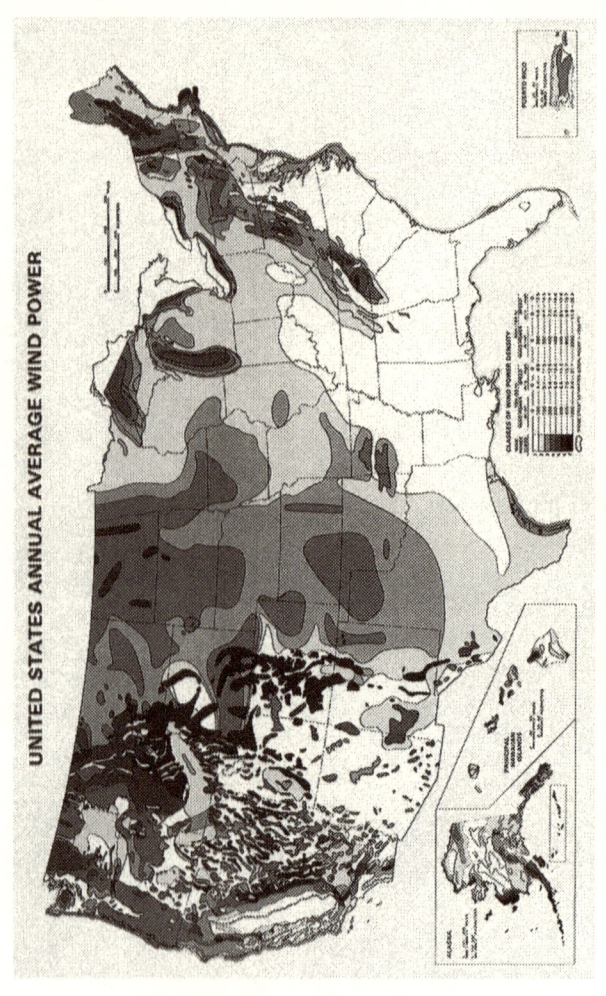

Figure 28 – Wind Power Map of the United States

Wind is the result of uneven solar heating of the earth's surface, which is in turn caused by the variation of sunlight intensity with latitude and irregular features of the land surface, cloud cover, etc. Amazingly, a tremendous amount of solar energy becomes wind – between 50 and 100 times as much energy as is converted into biomass by all the plants on earth through photosynthesis[93]! Wind energy is generally more intense at higher altitudes. **Figure 28** shows the average annual intensity of wind power throughout the United States, where the darker shades represent higher average wind intensities[94].

Wind power is a function of the size of the wind turbine and the cube of the wind speed. In other words, if the wind speed doubles, the power increases by a factor of eight (two cubed). Because of this relationship, short bursts of high-velocity wind contribute significantly to the total power generated by wind turbines.

Advantages of wind power include the following:

- Wind turbines require no fuel for operation, so there are no emissions to contribute to pollution or climate change.

- Wind is a renewable resource.

- Wind energy can be produced domestically.

- Wind energy is one of the lowest-priced renewable energy technologies available today, costing between $0.04 and $0.06 per kilowatt-hour, depending upon the wind resource and financing of the particular project[95].

- Wind turbines can benefit the economy in rural areas, where most of the best wind sites are found. Furthermore, land owners can generally continue to

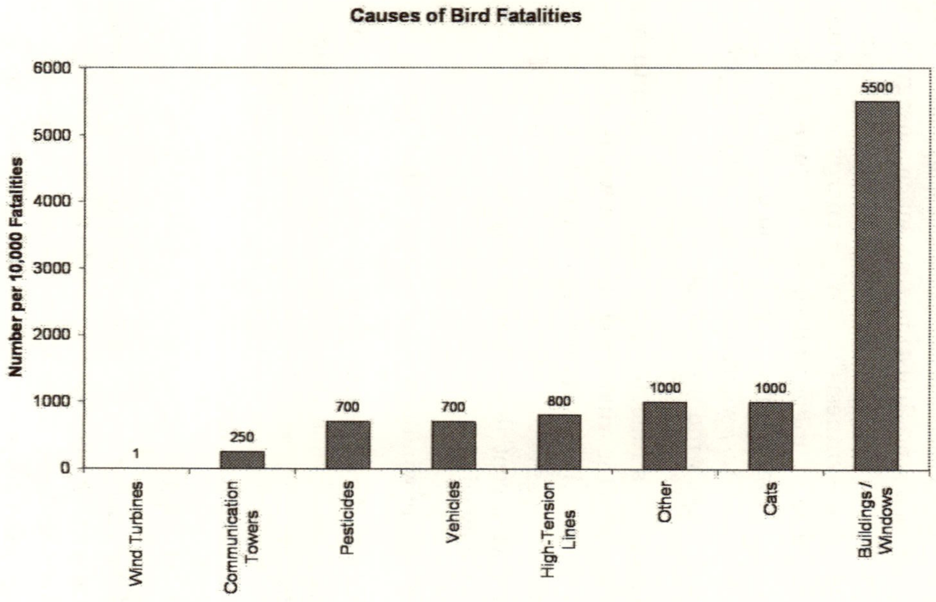

Causes of Bird Fatalities

Wind Turbines	1
Communication Towers	250
Pesticides	700
Vehicles	700
High-Tension Lines	800
Other	1000
Cats	1000
Buildings / Windows	5500

Number per 10,000 Fatalities

Figure 29 – Causes of Bird Fatalities

use the land for its original purpose because the wind turbines occupy little space.

Disadvantages of wind power include the following:

- Wind energy is intermittent, making it less suitable for base power loads. One strategy for mitigating this shortcoming is to use wind power to pump water to elevated storage, and use the resulting hydroelectric power as needed. However, this approach involves an additional energy conversion step, which (of course) costs efficiency.

- Some consider large wind turbines to be unsightly.

- High-wind areas tend to be located far from energy demand, raising the cost of transmission.

- Wind turbines have a reputation for being dangerous to wildlife such as birds and bats. However, this risk is relatively small compared to others (see **Figure 29**)[96].

Good wind areas, which cover 6% of the contiguous U.S. land area, have the potential to supply more than one and a half times the current electricity consumption of the United States[97].

Hydroelectric Power

The term "hydroelectric power" (or "hydro") generally refers to the process of allowing dammed (elevated) water to flow downhill, drive a turbine, and generate electricity. The water may gain its elevation through natural contours in the landscape, as is the case at Niagara Falls, or it may be pumped into an elevated reservoir as a means of storing energy for use during peak demand hours. In the case of naturally flowing water, the source of the energy is sunlight, which evaporates moisture at lower elevations and re-deposits it at higher elevations in the form of precipitation.

Many nations have fairly advanced hydro programs, including Canada, which generates 70% of its electricity from hydroelectric sources. In fact, hydroelectric power is so prominent in many parts of the country that the term "hydro" is used to refer to all electricity delivered by an electric utility, regardless of the method of generation[98]. **Figure 30** shows the hydroelectric power generators at Hoover Dam[99].

Figure 30 – Electric Power Generators at Hoover Dam

The advantages of hydro power include:

- Hydro systems require no fuel for operation, so there are no emissions to contribute to pollution or climate change.

- Naturally flowing water is a renewable resource.

- Hydro power can be produced domestically.

- Hydro power lends itself very well to storage and load balancing.

- Creation of recreational lakes.

The main disadvantages are:

- Damming of water may disrupt adjacent ecosystems, including fish populations and downstream erosion / deposition processes.

- The creation of reservoir lakes may force the relocation of local residents.

Geothermal Energy

The term "geothermal energy" refers to harnessing the natural heat of the earth's interior (mainly in the form of steam or hot water) to generate electricity or perform other useful work. Current technologies fall into three categories[100]:

- Dry steam plants, which directly use geothermal steam to turn turbines.

- Flash steam plants, which pull deep, high-pressure hot water into lower-pressure tanks and use the resulting flashed steam to drive turbines.

- Binary-cycle plants, which pass moderately hot geothermal water by a secondary fluid with a much lower boiling point than water. This causes the secondary fluid to flash to vapor, which then drives the turbines.

Although geothermal resources are virtually limitless, **Figure 5** shows that geothermal technologies represent only a fraction of a percent of the total U.S. energy consumption.

The benefits of geothermal energy include:

- Geothermal systems do not burn fossil fuels during operation, so they are inherently quite clean. They produce only about one-sixth of the carbon dioxide that a relatively clean natural-gas-fueled power plant produces, and very little if any, of the nitrous oxide or sulfur-bearing gases. Binary plants, which are closed cycle operations, release essentially no emissions[101].

- Geothermal energy offers very consistent output. Geothermal power plants have average availabilities of 90% or higher, compared to about 75% for coal plants[102].

- Geothermal power can be produced domestically. **Figure 31** shows the locations of geothermal resources in the U.S.[103]

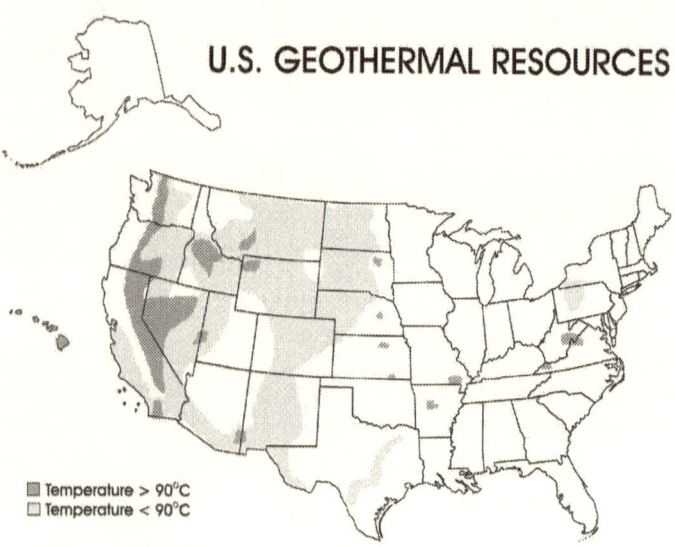

Figure 31 – U.S. Geothermal Resources

- The heat source for geothermal energy is the almost unlimited amount of heat generated by the Earth's core. Even in geothermal areas dependent on a reservoir of hot water, the volume taken out can be reinjected, making it a sustainable energy source[104].

The cost of geothermal energy is quite competitive - at The Geysers power plant in California, electricity is sold at $0.03 to $0.035 per kWh. A power plant built today would probably require about $0.05 per kWh[105].

Chapter 6: A Household Perspective

"I had three chairs in my house: one for solitude, two for friendship, three for society."

- Henry David Thoreau

So far, we have adopted a big-picture perspective throughout our discussion – in other words, we have focused on energy issues at a national or international level. However, most day-to-day consumption decisions are made by individuals or families at the household level. For this reason, we now attempt to develop an overview of the energy usage in American households, with the intent of summarizing the options available to bring about change.

Energy Consumption and Expenditures

The U.S. Department of Energy periodically conducts comprehensive surveys on household energy consumption. **Figure 32** shows the results of the 2001 survey categorized by household income level[106]. The most important categories of energy usage are vehicle fuel and space heating, and the importance of vehicle fuel climbs as income rises. Several factors probably contribute to this trend, including a higher rate of vehicle ownership in wealthier families (98% of households earning $50,000 or more, compared to 53% of households earning less than $10,000), lower fuel economy of luxury cars, and a greater distance traveled at higher incomes (roughly 30,000 miles annually for the wealthiest families vs. 13,000 miles for the poorest).

The values shown in **Figure 32** do not include energy that is consumed as a direct result of household choices, but is actually expended remotely from the home. For example, all other things being equal, a household that only drinks tap water consumes less energy than one that drinks Perrier water imported from France. A bottle of Perrier water "contains" a large amount of energy associated with its extraction, bottling, and transportation. For products that are processed within the U.S., this "hidden" energy shows up in the "commercial", "industrial", and "transportation" sectors of **Figure 4**. For imported products (such as Perrier water), the hidden energy

95

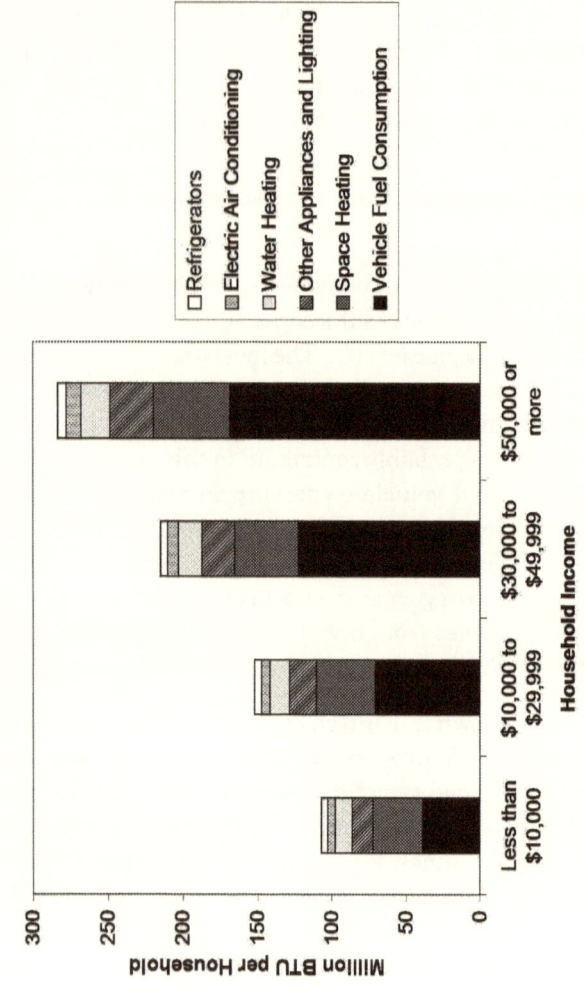

Figure 32 - Total Energy Consumption in U.S. Households

96

content only appears in the usage statistics of the source country.

Environmental Impact

Several publicly-available online tools allow individual consumers and households to estimate the environmental impact of their energy choices. British Petroleum's corporate website, http://www.bp.com, contains a carbon calculator that is a good example of such a tool. It allows the user to enter data about the number of people living in the household, the type of space heating system, distances traveled for personal and business trips, etc. The output is an estimate of the annual household carbon emissions, including a breakdown by source and a comparison to national averages (see **Figure 33**)[107].

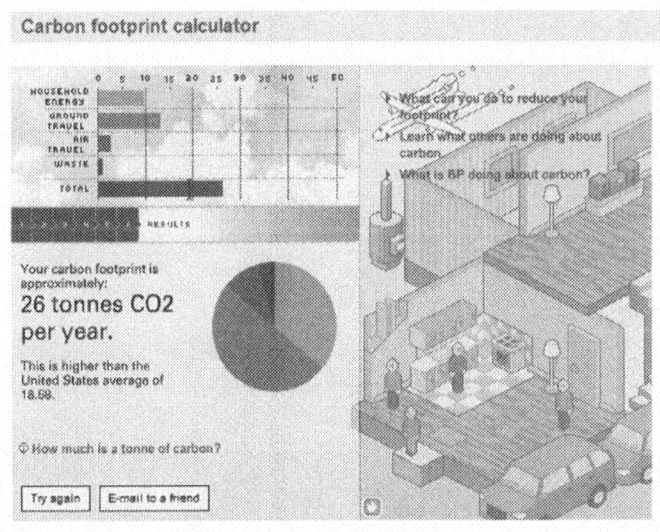

Figure 33 - Screen Capture from bp.com Carbon Calculator

Options for Change

If you want to change the way that your household consumes energy, the first step is to understand <u>why</u> you want to change. This is important because your answer to this question will determine the most effective strategy for your own personal situation. For example, if you simply want to spend less money on energy, you would do well to study your energy expenditures and focus on the areas that cost the most. Similarly, if your goal is to help reduce our nation's dependence on foreign oil, it doesn't make much sense to reduce your electricity consumption since less than 3% of oil goes towards electric power generation (see **Figure 6**).

However, regardless of your personal motives, options to change energy consumption generally fall into one of several broad categories:

1. Conservation – finding ways to use less energy to accomplish the same tasks, or in other words, reducing waste. For most households, this represents the most significant and cost-effective (albeit perhaps unglamorous) opportunity for change. For transportation-focused efforts, this might mean:

     a. Living closer to work

     b. Obeying the speed limit, since fuel economy rapidly decreases at speeds above 60 mph (see **Figure 34**)[108].

     c. Driving a more fuel-efficient car (or using public transportation).

     d. Walking or biking instead of driving

     e. Consolidating trips

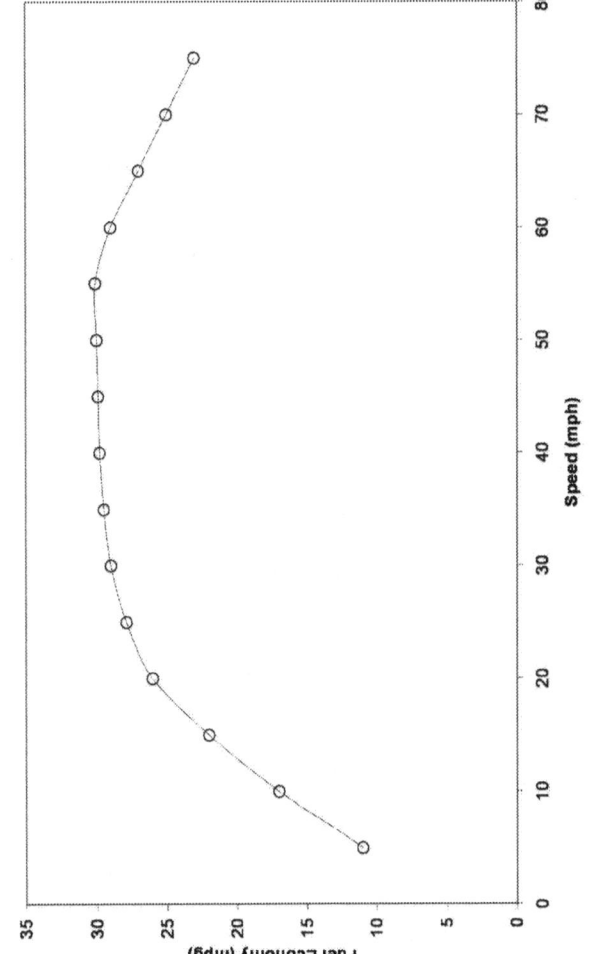

Figure 34 - Fuel Economy vs. Speed

For household-electricity (or other space heating fuel) conservation, options include:

    a. Improving insulation

    b. Purchasing energy efficient windows

    c. Purchasing energy efficient light bulbs

    d. Using a programmable thermostat to reduce over-heating and over-cooling when your home is unoccupied

The U.S. Department of Energy maintains some excellent on-line resources for improving household energy efficiency on the "For Consumers" section of their website – see for example, http://hes.lbl.gov/hes/answerdesk.html, "The Home Energy Saver Answer Desk".

2. Investing in alternative energy technologies. For transportation, this translates to:

    a. Purchasing a gas-electric hybrid vehicle

    b. Purchasing an E85 (ethanol) flex-fuel vehicle

    c. Using an alternative fuel such as biodiesel in a conventional diesel engine

Again, the U.S. Department of Energy offers valuable information for consumers on the "For Consumers" section of their website: http://www.doe.gov/yourcar.htm.

For home energy usage, there are several options for investing in alternative energy technologies:

    a. Purchasing "green energy" from your local utility. This involves paying a premium on your electric bills for your utility to deliver electricity from renewable sources via the traditional wires infrastructure. In principle, this type of investment should reduce the cost of developing renewable electricity faster than would otherwise happen. To date, more than 600 utilities, including investor-owned companies, municipal utilities, and cooperatives, offer a green pricing option. **Figure 35** shows a summary by state.

Utility Green Pricing Activities

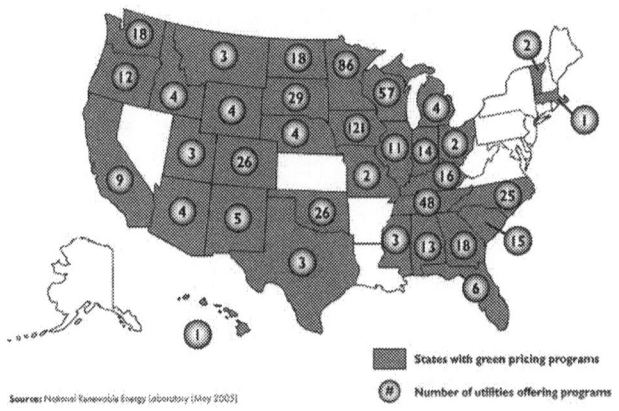

Sources: National Renewable Energy Laboratory (May 2005)

■ States with green pricing programs

(#) Number of utilities offering programs

Figure 35 – Green Energy Pricing Options by State

b. Installing alternative energy technology in your home. In such an arrangement (let's say you install solar electric panels on your roof), the renewable energy is generated on your property rather than at your utility's power plant. Nevertheless, in almost all cases, your home would still be connected to the power grid. This connection serves two purposes: (1) to allow you to purchase electricity from your utility during times when your household demand exceeds the capacity of the solar electric system, and (2) to allow you to sell electricity back to the grid when your solar system generates a surplus of electricity.

The most popular arrangement for this type of connection to the utility grid is called "net metering". With net metering, your home uses a single electricity meter that measures the "net" amount of electricity that the utility sells to your home. In cases when you sell power back to the grid, the meter actually spins backwards. This arrangement has the advantage of giving the consumer full market price for the electricity sold. At least 35 states currently offer some type of net metering arrangement, and many of them legally require utilities to participate.

The Department of Energy's Office of Energy Efficiency and Renewable Energy maintains a list of net metering programs offered in each state at: http://www.eere.energy.gov/greenpower/markets/netmetering.shtml.

Chapter 7: Ten Questions for You to Consider When Developing an Informed Opinion

"Someone told me that each equation I included in the book would halve the sales."

- Stephen Hawking

If you recall from the foreword, the purpose of this book is to "provide you with a non-partisan layperson's guide to energy issues currently facing the U.S., with a view towards helping you to become an informed 'consumer' of energy policy". You have now completed the guided tour. The last step is to for you to perform some self-analysis and introspection to develop a clear understanding of your own opinions on energy issues. The following list of questions is intended to prompt you in this effort. If you consider them carefully and develop the answers for yourself, you should be well prepared to face (and shape) our nation's energy future.

1. Considering America's energy usage and the associated consequences, what degree of change, if any, do you feel is necessary?

2. If change is required, what should be our top two or three national energy priorities?

3. To what extent should we rely on market forces, government policy, or both to bring about these changes?

4. Returning to **Figure 5 – 2005 U.S. Total Energy Consumption by Fuel Type**, what should this picture look like five years from now? Ten years from now? Fifty years from now?

5. What priority and funding should energy issues receive compared to other issues of national significance, such as health care, defense, education, etc.?

6. How much emphasis should be placed on improving traditional energy technologies (e.g., fewer emissions from coal power plants) vs. developing alternative technologies?

7. Which alternative energy sources appear to be the most promising?

8. To what extent should the U.S. join forces with other nations and international bodies to solve energy problems?

9. What personal choices can you make in your daily life to positively impact our energy situation?

10. Should emerging economies be held to the same standard of energy responsibility as developed economies, given our own country's history of energy choices?

ENDNOTES

[1] United Nations. United Nations Framework Convention on Climate Change. Kyoto Protocol, Status of Ratification. 18 Apr. 2006. 08 May 2006 <http://unfccc.int/files/essential_background/kyoto_protocol/application/pdf/kpstats.pdf>.

[2] "State of the Union Address by the President." The White House - George W. Bush. 31 Jan. 2006. 06 May 2006 <http://www.whitehouse.gov/stateoftheunion/2006/index.html>.

[3] "Granholm Announces Online Petition Asking President Bush to Help Lower Gas Prices." Office of the Governor - Governor Jennifer M. Granholm. 21 Apr. 2006. State of Michigan. 06 May 2006 <http://www.michigan.gov/gov/0,1607,7-168-23442-141527--,00.html>.

[4] United States of America. National Energy Policy Development Group. Reliable, Affordable, and Environmentally Sound Energy for America's Future. May 2001. 01 May 2006 <http://www.whitehouse.gov/energy/>.

[5] United States of America. Central Intelligence Agency. The World Factbook. 02 May 2006. 08 May 2006 <http://www.cia.gov/cia/publications/factbook/geos/us.html>.

[6] "GDP Vs. Energy Efficiency." Chart. Peter Corless. 10 May 2006 <http://en.wikipedia.org/wiki/Image:Gdp-energy-efficiency.jpg>.

[7] International Energy Agency. Energy Balances of OECD Countries (2003 Edition) and Energy Balances of Non-OECD Countries (2003 Edition). 09 May 2006 <http://data.iea.org/ieastore/default.asp>.

[8] United States of America. Energy Information Administration. Department of Energy. Monthly Energy Review. Apr. 2006. 10 May 2006 <http://www.eia.doe.gov/emeu/mer/pdf/pages/sec2_3.pdf>.

[9] United States of America. Energy Information Administration. Department of Energy. Monthly Energy Review. Apr. 2006. 10 May 2006 <http://www.eia.doe.gov/emeu/mer/pdf/pages/sec1_7.pdf>.

[10] United States of America. Energy Information Administration. Department of Energy. Annual Energy Review. 15 Mar. 2006. 08 May 2006 <http://www.eia.doe.gov/emeu/aer/pdf/pages/sec5_3.pdf>.

[11] United States of America. Energy Information Administration. Department of Energy. Annual Energy Review. 15 Mar. 2006. 08 May 2006 <http://tonto.eia.doe.gov/dnav/pet/pet_move_impcus_a2_nus_ep00_im0_mbbl_a.htm>.

[12] United States of America. Energy Information Administration. Department of Energy. U.S. Coal Supply and Demand, 2005 Review. Apr. 2006. 08 May 2006 <http://www.eia.doe.gov/cneaf/coal/page/special/feature.html>.

[13] United States of America. Energy Information Administration. Department of Energy. International Natural Gas and Liquefied Natural Gas (LNG) Imports and Exports. 08 May 2006 <http://www.eia.doe.gov/emeu/international/gastrade.html>.

[14] International Atomic Energy Agency. <u>Implementation of the NPT Safeguards Agreement in the Islamic Republic of Iran Resolution Adopted on 4 February 2006</u>. 04 Feb. 2006. 09 Mar. 2006 <<u>http://www.iaea.org/Publications/Documents/Board/2006/gov2006-14.pdf</u>>.

[15] International Atomic Energy Agency. <u>Chernobyl 20 Years Later: an IAEA in Focus Series</u>. 09 Mar. 2006 <<u>http://www.iaea.org/NewsCenter/Focus/Chernobyl/index.html</u>>.

[16] "Greenpeace Rejects Chernobyl Toll." <u>BBC News</u> 18 Apr. 2006. 10 May 2006 <<u>http://news.bbc.co.uk/1/hi/world/europe/4917526.stm</u>>.

[17] "Nuclear Fuel Cycle." <u>Wikipedia</u>. 03 May 2006. 10 May 2006 <<u>http://en.wikipedia.org/wiki/Nuclear_fuel_cycle</u>>.

[18] United States of America. Bureau of Transportation Statistics. Department of Transportation. <u>National Transportation Statistics</u>. 2004. 08 May 2006 <<u>http://www.bts.gov/publications/national_transportation_statistics/html/table_02_01.html</u>>.

[19] United States of America. Nuclear Regulatory Commission. Department of Energy. <u>Fact Sheet on the Accident At Three Mile Island</u>. 27 Mar. 2006. 10 May 2006 <<u>http://www.nrc.gov/reading-rm/doc-collections/fact-sheets/3mile-isle.html</u>>.

[20] <u>Information and Issue Briefs, Three Mile Island: 1979</u>. World Nuclear Association. 2001. 07 May 2006 <<u>http://www.world-nuclear.org/info/inf36.htm</u>>.

[21] "World Nuclear Power Reactors 2004-2006 and Uranium Requirements." <u>Uranium Information Centre</u> 31 Mar. 2006. 10 May 2006 <<u>http://www.uic.com.au/reactors.htm</u>>.

[22] United States of America. Energy Information Administration. Department of Energy. International Petroleum (Oil) Stocks. 08 May 2006 <http://www.eia.doe.gov/emeu/international/oilstocks.html>.

[23] United States of America. National Hydrogen Vision Meeting. Department of Energy. Toward a More Secure and Cleaner Energy Future for America; a National Vision of America's Transition to a Hydrogen Economy - to 2030 and Beyond. Feb. 2002. 13 May 2006 <http://www1.eere.energy.gov/hydrogenandfuelcells/pdfs/vision_doc.pdf>.

[24] "Iraq War Could Cost $2.6 Trillion." The Age 10 Jan. 2006. 06 May 2006 <http://www.theage.com.au/news/world/iraq-war-could-cost-26-trillion/2006/01/10/1136851198921.html>.

[25] "Real Cost of Oil Equates to $10 Gallon Gasoline." EV World 02 Apr. 2006. 11 May 2006 <http://www.evworld.com/view.cfm?section=communique&newsid=11520&url=>.

[26] United Nations. Intergovernmental Panel on Climate Change. United Nations Environmental Programme. Climate Change 2001: Working Group I: the Scientific Basis. 08 May 2006 <http://www.grida.no/climate/ipcc_tar/wg1/007.htm>.

[27] United Nations. Intergovernmental Panel on Climate Change. United Nations Environmental Programme. Climate Change 2001: Working Group I: the Scientific Basis. 08 May 2006 <http://www.grida.no/climate/ipcc_tar/wg1/007.htm>.

[28] Barnola, J.m., D. Raynaud, C. Lorius, and N.i. Barkov. United States of America. Oak Ridge National Laboratory. Department of Energy. Historical CO_2 Record From the Vostok Ice Core. in Trends: a

Compendium of Data on Global Change. 2003. 13 May 2006 <http://cdiac.esd.ornl.gov/trends/co2/vostok.htm>.

[29] Keeling, C.d., and T.p. Whorf. United States of America. Oak Ridge National Laboratory. Department of Energy. Atmospheric CO2 Records From Sites in the SIO Air Sampling Network. in Trends: a Compendium of Data on Global Change. 2005. 13 May 2006 <http://cdiac.ornl.gov/trends/co2/sio-mlo.htm>.

[30] Kargel, Jeffrey. United States of America. Visible Earth. National Aeronautics and Space Administration. Glacial Lakes From Retreating Glaciers. 04 June 2002. 09 May 2006 <http://visibleearth.nasa.gov/view_rec.php?id=2876>.

[31] Kargel, Jeffrey. United States of America. Visible Earth. National Aeronautics and Space Administration. Glacial Lakes From Retreating Glaciers. 04 June 2002. 09 May 2006 <http://visibleearth.nasa.gov/view_rec.php?id=2876>.

[32] United States of America. Geophysical Fluid Dynamics Laboratory. National Oceanic and Atmospheric Administration. 11 May 2006 <http://www.gfdl.noaa.gov/products/vis/images/gallery/sea-ice_1950s-2050s.gif>.

[33] United States of America. National Energy Technology Laboratory. Department of Energy. Carbon Sequestration. 11 May 2006 <http://www.netl.doe.gov/technologies/carbon_seq/core_rd/storage.html>.

[34] Bell, Michelle L. "Ozone and Short-Term Mortality in 95 US Urban Communities, 1987-2000." Journal of the American Medical Association 292 (2004). 11 May 2006 <http://jama.ama-assn.org/cgi/content/short/292/19/2372>.

[35] Gabbard, Alex. United States of America. Oak Ridge National Laboratory. Department of Energy. Coal

Combustion: Nuclear Resource or Danger. 7 May 2006
<http://www.ornl.gov/info/ornlreview/rev26-34/text/
colmain.html>.

[36] Gabbard, Alex. United States of America. Oak Ridge
National Laboratory. Department of Energy. Coal
Combustion: Nuclear Resource or Danger. 7 May 2006
<http://www.ornl.gov/info/ornlreview/rev26-34/text/
colmain.html>.

[37] Gabbard, Alex. United States of America. Oak Ridge
National Laboratory. Department of Energy. Coal
Combustion: Nuclear Resource or Danger. 7 May 2006
<http://www.ornl.gov/info/ornlreview/rev26-34/text/
colmain.html>.

[38] Gabbard, Alex. United States of America. Oak Ridge
National Laboratory. Department of Energy. Coal
Combustion: Nuclear Resource or Danger. 7 May 2006
<http://www.ornl.gov/info/ornlreview/rev26-34/text/
colmain.html>.

[39] United States of America. Energy Information
Administration. Department of Energy. U.S. Coal
Supply and Demand, 2005 Review. Apr. 2006. 08 May
2006 <http://www.eia.doe.gov/emeu/international/
contents.html>.

[40] "Hubbert Peak Theory." Wikipedia. 11 May 2006. 10
May 2006 <http://en.wikipedia.org/wiki/Peak_oil>.

[41] United States of America. Central Intelligence
Agency. The World Factbook. 06 May 2006. 12 May
2006 <http://www.cia.gov/cia/publications/factbook/geos/
fr.html#Econ>.

[42] Doyle, Michelle. "Police Fire Rubber Bullets At
Crowds as Paris Labour Law Protest Turns Into Riot."
Guardian Unlimited 17 Mar. 2006. 12 May 2006 <http://
www.guardian.co.uk/france/story/0,,1733125,00.html>.

[43] United States of America. Department of Energy. Federal Income Tax Incentives for Hybrid Vehicle Purchases. 12 May 2006 <http://www.fueleconomy.gov/feg/tax_hybrid.shtml>.

[44] United States of America. National Highway Traffic Safety Administration. Department of Transportation. Summary of Fuel Economy Performance. Mar. 2004. 12 May 2006 <http://www.nhtsa.gov/cars/rules/CAFE/docs/Summary-Fuel-Economy-Pref-2004.pdf>.

[45] United States of America. Bureau of Transportation Statistics. Department of Transportation. National Transportation Statistics. 2004. 12 May 2006 <http://www.bts.gov/publications/national_transportation_statistics/html/table_01_37.html>.

[46] United States of America. Bureau of Transportation Statistics. Department of Transportation. National Transportation Statistics. 2004. 12 May 2006 <http://www.bts.gov/publications/national_transportation_statistics/html/table_04_05.html>.

[47] United States of America. United States Census Bureau. United States Census 2000. 25 June 2002. 12 May 2006 <http://www.census.gov/main/www/cen2000.html>.

[48] "International Urban Rail: Passengers Per Line Mile." Public Purpose. 13 May 2006 <www.publicpurpose.com/ut-wrail.htm>.

[49] "Arctic Refuge Drilling Controversy." Wikipedia. 11 May 2006. 13 May 2006 <http://en.wikipedia.org/wiki/Arctic_Refuge_drilling_controversy>.

[50] United States of America. United States Geological Survey. Department of the Interior. Arctic National Wildlife Refuge, 1002 Area, Petroleum Assessment, 1998, Including Economic Analysis. Apr. 2001. 13

May 2006 <http://pubs.usgs.gov/fs/fs-0028-01/fs-0028-01.pdf>.

[51] United States of America. Senate Committee on Energy & Natural Resources. Energy Conference Update #21 (Fake Jobs Vs. Real Jobs). 22 Oct. 2003. 13 May 2006 <http://energy.senate.gov/public/index.cfm?FuseAction=PressReleases.Detail&PressRelease_id=621&Month=10&Year=2003&Party=0>.

[52] United States of America. U.S. Fish & Wildlife Service - Alaska. Department of the Interior. Arctic National Wildlife Refuge, Wild Lands, Ecological Regions with a Focus on the Coastal Plain and Foothills. 14 Feb. 2003. 13 May 2006 <http://arctic.fws.gov/ecoregions.htm>.

[53] United States of America. Department of Energy. FutureGen - Tomorrow's Pollution-Free Power Plant. 27 Feb. 2003. 12 May 2006 <http://www.fossil.energy.gov/programs/powersystems/futuregen/>.

[54] "Nuclear Poison." Wikipedia. 03 May 2006. 07 May 2006 <http://en.wikipedia.org/wiki/Nuclear_poison>.

[55] "Spent Fuel Pool." Wikipedia. 07 Mar. 2006. 13 May 2006 <http://en.wikipedia.org/wiki/Spent_fuel_pool>.

[56] United States of America. U.S. Senate Committee on Environment and Public Works Majority Staff. Yucca Mountain: the Most Studied Real Estate on the Planet. Mar. 2006. 13 May 2006 <http://epw.senate.gov/repwhitepapers/YuccaMountainEPWReport.pdf>.

[57] "Yucca Mountain." Wikipedia. 12 May 2006. 13 May 2006 <http://en.wikipedia.org/wiki/Yucca_Mountain>.

[58] United States of America. U.S. Senate Committee on Environment and Public Works Majority Staff. Yucca Mountain: the Most Studied Real Estate on the Planet. Mar. 2006. 13 May 2006 <http://epw.senate.gov/repwhitepapers/YuccaMountainEPWReport.pdf>.

[59] United States of America. National Renewable Energy Laboratory. Department of Energy. Best Research Cell Efficiencies. 07 May 2006 <http://www.nrel.gov/ncpv/thin_film/docs/kaz_best_research_cells.ppt>.

[60] "Solar Power." Wikipedia. 12 May 2006. 12 May 2006 <http://en.wikipedia.org/wiki/Solar_power#Compact_systems>.

[61] "FPL Energy Portfolio." 12 May 2006 <http://www.fplenergy.com/portfolio/contents/segs_viii.shtml>.

[62] United States of America. Energy Efficiency and Renewable Energy. Department of Energy. Fuel Cell Overview. 13 May 2006 <http://www.eere.energy.gov/hydrogenandfuelcells/education/pdfs/fuel_cell_facts.pdf>.

[63] United States of America. National Hydrogen Vision Meeting. Department of Energy. Toward a More Secure and Cleaner Energy Future for America; a National Vision of America's Transition to a Hydrogen Economy - to 2030 and Beyond. Feb. 2002. 13 May 2006 <http://www1.eere.energy.gov/hydrogenandfuelcells/pdfs/vision_doc.pdf>.

[64] "Fuel Cell." Wikipedia. 13 May 2006. 13 May 2006 <http://en.wikipedia.org/wiki/Fuel_cell>.

[65] United States of America. National Hydrogen Vision Meeting. Department of Energy. Toward a More Secure and Cleaner Energy Future for America; a National Vision of America's Transition to a Hydrogen Economy - to 2030 and Beyond. Feb. 2002. 13 May 2006 <http://www1.eere.energy.gov/hydrogenandfuelcells/pdfs/vision_doc.pdf>.

[66] United States of America. National Hydrogen Vision Meeting. Department of Energy. Toward a More Secure and Cleaner Energy Future for America; a National Vision of America's Transition to a Hydrogen Economy

- to 2030 and Beyond. Feb. 2002. 13 May 2006 <http://
www1.eere.energy.gov/hydrogenandfuelcells/pdfs/vision_
doc.pdf>.

[67] United States of America. National Hydrogen Vision
Meeting. Department of Energy. _Toward a More Secure
and Cleaner Energy Future for America; a National
Vision of America's Transition to a Hydrogen Economy
- to 2030 and Beyond_. Feb. 2002. 13 May 2006 <http://
www1.eere.energy.gov/hydrogenandfuelcells/pdfs/vision_
doc.pdf>.

[68] United States of America. National Hydrogen Vision
Meeting. Department of Energy. _Toward a More Secure
and Cleaner Energy Future for America; a National
Vision of America's Transition to a Hydrogen Economy
- to 2030 and Beyond_. Feb. 2002. 13 May 2006 <http://
www1.eere.energy.gov/hydrogenandfuelcells/pdfs/vision_
doc.pdf>.

[69] United States of America. Energy Efficiency and
Renewable Energy. Department of Energy. _Hydrogen,
Fuel Cells & Infrastructure_. 13 May 2006 <http://www.
eere.energy.gov/hydrogenandfuelcells/fuelcells/basics.
html>.

[70] United States of America. National Hydrogen Vision
Meeting. Department of Energy. _Toward a More Secure
and Cleaner Energy Future for America; a National
Vision of America's Transition to a Hydrogen Economy
- to 2030 and Beyond_. Feb. 2002. 13 May 2006 <http://
www1.eere.energy.gov/hydrogenandfuelcells/pdfs/vision_
doc.pdf>.

[71] "Fuel Cell." _Wikipedia_. 13 May 2006. 13 May 2006
<http://en.wikipedia.org/wiki/Fuel_cell>.

[72] United States of America. Energy Efficiency and
Renewable Energy. Department of Energy. _Fuel Cell
Overview_. 13 May 2006 <http://www.eere.energy.gov/

hydrogenandfuelcells/education/pdfs/fuel_cell_facts.
pdf>.

[73] United States of America. Energy Efficiency and
Renewable Energy. Department of Energy. Fuel Cell
Overview. 13 May 2006 <http://www.eere.energy.gov/
hydrogenandfuelcells/education/pdfs/fuel_cell_facts.
pdf>.

[74] "Agricultural Subsidy." Wikipedia. 14 May 2006. 16
May 2006 <http://en.wikipedia.org/wiki/Agricultural_
subsidies>.

[75] Net Energy Balance of Ethanol Production. Ethanol
Across America. 15 May 2006 <http://www.ethanol.org/
documents/NetEnergyBalanceissuebrief.pdf>.

[76] United States of America. National Biomass Initiative.
Department of Energy. The U.S. Dry Mill Ethanol
Industry. 16 May 2006 <http://www.biomass.govtools.
us/pdfs/drymill_ethanol_industry.pdf>.

[77] United States of America. Energy Information
Administration. Department of Energy. Outlook for
Biomass Ethanol Production and Demand. 18 May 2006
<http://www.eia.doe.gov/oiaf/analysispaper/biomass.
html>.

[78] United States of America. Energy Information
Administration. Department of Energy. Outlook for
Biomass Ethanol Production and Demand. 18 May 2006
<http://www.eia.doe.gov/oiaf/analysispaper/biomass.
html>.

[79] United States of America. Energy Information
Administration. Department of Energy. Outlook for
Biomass Ethanol Production and Demand. 18 May 2006
<http://www.eia.doe.gov/oiaf/analysispaper/biomass.
html>.

[80] United States of America. Energy Efficiency and Renewable Energy. Department of Energy. Net Energy Balance for Bioethanol Production and Use. 16 May 2006 <http://www1.eere.energy.gov/biomass/net_energy_balance.html>.

[81] "Fossil Fuel Power Plant." Wikipedia. 16 May 2006. 16 May 2006 <http://en.wikipedia.org/wiki/Coal_power_plant>.

[82] United States of America. Energy Efficiency and Renewable Energy. Department of Energy. Net Energy Balance for Bioethanol Production and Use. 16 May 2006 <http://www1.eere.energy.gov/biomass/net_energy_balance.html>.

[83] Sheehan, John, Vince Camobreco, James Duffield, Michael Graboski, and Housein Shapouri. United States of America. National Renewable Energy Laboratory. Department of Agriculture and Department of Energy. An Overview of Biodiesel and Petroleum Life Cycles. May 1998. 16 May 2006 <http://devafdc.nrel.gov/pdfs/3812.pdf>.

[84] Sheehan, John, Vince Camobreco, James Duffield, Michael Graboski, and Housein Shapouri. United States of America. National Renewable Energy Laboratory. Department of Agriculture and Department of Energy. An Overview of Biodiesel and Petroleum Life Cycles. May 1998. 16 May 2006 <http://devafdc.nrel.gov/pdfs/3812.pdf>.

[85] "Agricultural Subsidy." Wikipedia. 14 May 2006. 16 May 2006 <http://en.wikipedia.org/wiki/Agricultural_subsidies>.

[86] Sheehan, John, Vince Camobreco, James Duffield, Michael Graboski, and Housein Shapouri. United States of America. National Renewable Energy Laboratory. Department of Agriculture and Department of Energy.

An Overview of Biodiesel and Petroleum Life Cycles.
May 1998. 16 May 2006 <http://devafdc.nrel.gov/
pdfs/3812.pdf>.

[87] "Biodiesel." Wikipedia. 18 May 2006. 18 May 2006
<http://en.wikipedia.org/wiki/Biodiesel>.

[88] "Biodiesel." Wikipedia. 18 May 2006. 18 May 2006
<http://en.wikipedia.org/wiki/Biodiesel>.

[89] "Biodiesel." Wikipedia. 18 May 2006. 18 May 2006
<http://en.wikipedia.org/wiki/Biodiesel>.

[90] "Biodiesel Production and Quality." National Biodiesel
Board. 19 May 2006 <http://www.biodiesel.org/pdf_files/
fuelfactsheets/prod_quality.pdf>.

[91] Sheehan, John, Vince Camobreco, James Duffield,
Michael Graboski, and Housein Shapouri. United States
of America. National Renewable Energy Laboratory.
Department of Agriculture and Department of Energy.
An Overview of Biodiesel and Petroleum Life Cycles.
May 1998. 16 May 2006 <http://devafdc.nrel.gov/
pdfs/3812.pdf>.

[92] United States of America. Sandia National
Laboratories. Department of Energy. Sandia
Researchers Seek Ways to Lower the Cost of Wind
Energy. 29 Sept. 2003. 19 May 2006 <http://www.
sandia.gov/news-center/news-releases/2003/renew-
energy-batt/wind-turbines.html>.

[93] "Biodiesel." Wikipedia. 19 May 2006. 19 May 2006
<http://en.wikipedia.org/wiki/Wind_power>.

[94] United States of America. Renewable Resource Data
Center. Department of Energy. United States Annual
Average Wind Power. 19 May 2006 <http://rredc.nrel.
gov/wind/pubs/atlas/maps/chap2/2-01m.html>.

[95] United States of America. Energy Efficiency and Renewable Energy. Department of Energy. <u>Advantages and Disadvantages of Wind Energy</u>. 30 Aug. 2005. 19 May 2006 <<u>http://eereweb.ee.doe.gov/windandhydro/wind_ad.html</u>>.

[96] "Windpower Outlook 2006." American Wind Energy Association. 19 May 2006 <<u>http://www.osti.gov/bridge/servlets/purl/881759-4QHaLi/881759.PDF</u>>.

[97] United States of America. Energy Efficiency and Renewable Energy. Department of Energy. <u>Advantages and Disadvantages of Wind Energy</u>. 30 Aug. 2005. 19 May 2006 <<u>http://eereweb.ee.doe.gov/windandhydro/wind_ad.html</u>>.

[98] "Hydroelectricity." <u>Wikipedia</u>. 19 May 2006. 19 May 2006 <<u>http://en.wikipedia.org/wiki/Hydroelectricity</u>>.

[99] "Hydroelectric Generators Photo." <u>PD Photos</u>. 19 May 2006 <<u>http://pdphoto.org/PictureDetail.php?pg=8536</u>>.

[100] United States of America. Energy Efficiency and Renewable Energy. Department of Energy. <u>Geothermal FAQs</u>. 13 Jan. 2006. 19 May 2006 <<u>http://www1.eere.energy.gov/geothermal/faqs.html</u>>.

[101] United States of America. Energy Efficiency and Renewable Energy. Department of Energy. <u>Geothermal FAQs</u>. 13 Jan. 2006. 19 May 2006 <<u>http://www1.eere.energy.gov/geothermal/faqs.html</u>>.

[102] United States of America. Energy Efficiency and Renewable Energy. Department of Energy. <u>Geothermal FAQs</u>. 13 Jan. 2006. 19 May 2006 <<u>http://www1.eere.energy.gov/geothermal/faqs.html</u>>.

[103] "Transparent Energy Graphics." 19 May 2006 <<u>http://www.need.org/TransparentGraphics/</u>>.

[104] United States of America. Energy Efficiency and Renewable Energy. Department of Energy. Geothermal FAQs. 13 Jan. 2006. 19 May 2006 <http://www1.eere.energy.gov/geothermal/faqs.html>.

[105] United States of America. Energy Efficiency and Renewable Energy. Department of Energy. Geothermal FAQs. 13 Jan. 2006. 19 May 2006 <http://www1.eere.energy.gov/geothermal/faqs.html>.

[106] United States of America. Energy Information Administration. Department of Energy. A Look at Residential Energy Consumption in 2001. 25 May 2006 <http://www.eia.doe.gov/emeu/consumption>.

[107] "Environment and Society - Carbon Footprint Calculator." BP Global. 25 May 2006 <http://www.bp.com/extendedsectiongenericarticle.do?categoryId=9008204&contentId=7015209>.

[108] United States of America. Department of Energy. Tips to Improve Your Gas Mileage. 28 May 2006 <http://www.fueleconomy.gov/feg/driveHabits.shtml>.

ABOUT THE AUTHOR

Thomas G. Komjathy was educated at The University of Michigan, receiving a B.S.E. in Chemical Engineering and an M.B.A. from the Stephen M. Ross School of Business. He has engineering, logistics, and consulting experience in the chemical, pharmaceutical, and coatings industries. He is a licensed Professional Engineer in the State of Michigan and resides in the Detroit area with his family.

www.ingramcontent.com/pod-product-compliance
Lightning Source LLC
Chambersburg PA
CBHW020242290526
45784CB00003B/1079